Brain Friendly
Language Learning

Neurolanguage Coaching

Disclaimer

Any statements made in this book as to the neuroscientific research which supports Neurolanguage Coaching are made in good faith on the basis of the findings of published, peer-reviewed, scientific journals and books relating to neuroscience and brain related texts and articles at the time of publication and not any first-hand scientific research undertaken by the author herself. In the absence of any fraud or negligence, no responsibility for any errors or omissions, or loss or damage suffered by any person acting, or refraining from acting, as a result of the material in this publication, can be accepted by the publisher or the author.

Brain Friendly
Language Learning

Neurolanguage Coaching

RACHEL PALING

THE CHOIR PRESS

First published in the United Kingdom in 2017 by
The Choir Press

ISBN 978-1-910864-94-4

"Live as if you were to die tomorrow.
Learn as if you were to live forever."

– Mahatma Gandhi

Contents

Part V

Acknowledgements

I am especially grateful to all those language teachers who have certified with me over the past 3 years. They are the brave ones and the pioneers. Without them this concept would never have moved forward.

I would also like to thank Claudio Tambara, who supported me from the beginning, and who created the websites and artistic logo of Efficient Language Coaching. I had requested that Claudio think of a logo that portrayed the fleur-de-lis and he then created the shape designed before the ELC letters, which is in fact the combination of the letters E (on the left of the design) L (upper right) C (bottom right) together with the half fleur-de-lis. Some say it looks like a person giving something, others say it looks like a person bowing towards something.

Neurolanguage Coaching® is a registered trademark in Europe and the US. Efficient Language Coaching and ELC Language Coaching Certification are both European trademarks registered under Efficient Language Coaching. The 3Ms, the 5Cs, the PACT PQC model and the PROGRESS model are copyright of Rachel Marie Paling. All references in this book to Neurolanguage Coaching shall be made hereinafter without the ® symbol, under the tacit understanding that it refers to the trademark.

Introduction

I am not a neuroscientist. Nor do I profess to be one. Yet I have created a new concept called Neurolanguage Coaching, based on the introduction of the principles of neuroscience as well as the structure and principles of coaching in the language learning process.

So, who am I to say what Neurolanguage Coaching is?

The creation of this concept called Neurolanguage Coaching emerged through my own experience of teaching languages on and off over the last 32 years. This was combined with my own experience of learning languages, namely French, Spanish, Italian, German, and some Catalan, with basics of Arabic and Russian and hunger to learn more, such as Chinese. In addition, my own personal development as a life coach over the last eight years and my burning interest in what we are now discovering through modern neuroscience about the brain – and how the brain functions, reacts and learns – have all contributed to the creation of this concept. The most fascinating driver for me has been seeing and experiencing better learning results from my own clients. Now, also the testimonials of many of the language teachers who have certified with me and become Neurolanguage coaches, are, in turn, witnessing better results from their clients.

I am well aware that my explanations of the neuroscientific principles may well be a layman's (or rather laywoman's) interpretation and not an academic description, and even some may be my own speculative observations. However, my whole intuition leads me to interpret what is now being given to us as results from the neuroscience field, as well as quantum physics and epigenetics and our comprehension of how much we ourselves can empower and change our own brains, even to the extent of potentially influencing our external world. Let us consider the expression 'energy flows where attention goes' (and we will look at this in more depth later in the book). One of the frequent questions we should be asking our learner constantly is 'Where is your attention at the moment – what are you in fact focusing on right now – are you focusing on the positive of "yes, I can learn" or on the negative of "I will never learn"?'

Then, try to help clients understand that where they focus their attention, they will be reinforcing those 'brain connections' and neural networks. The more we focus our attention on something, the stronger the neural connections. Consider playing the piano: the more we practise, the more attention we pay on this activity, the more the brain connects and the piano playing improves. Interestingly we now know from the research that the brain does not in fact differentiate 'real performance of an activity' from 'thought only performance of an activity'.[1] This signifies that we can also strengthen neural networks and even increase muscle strength[2] only through the power of thought! Absolutely amazing! (Potentially also the topic of another book!)

I personally now am understanding so much more about my own brain and I am able to 'dominate' it. In addition, I would like to reach out to millions of you to help you also understand your own brains and to understand the amazing holistic system, connecting brain, heart and gut, that we all carry within us. Someone recently said to me, 'The brain is like a wild horse. You either learn to tame it, take the reins and control it, or it will constantly gallop along out of control, with you, the rider, trying to control it!' (a wonderful metaphor that originates from Tibetan Buddhist teachings).

Nevertheless, even neuroscience itself cannot be said to be 100% definite. Only over the last 30 years, modern technology has offered us

---

[1] Pascual-Leone, A., Nguyet, D., Cohen, L.G., Brasil-Neto, J.P. Cammerota, A., and Hallet, M. (1995) *Modulation of muscle responses evoked by transcranial magnetic stimulation during the acquisition of new fine motor skills*. Journal of Neurophysiology 74(3), 1037–1045.

[2] Ranganathan, V.K., Siemionow, V., Liu, J.Z., Sahgal, V., and Yue, G.H. (2004) *From mental power to muscle power: Gaining strength by using the mind*. Neuropsychologia 42(7), 944–56.

the amazing possibilities of actually 'seeing' the brain and how the brain works. However, a recent article[3] suggests that there could be a very serious problem with the past 15 years of research owing to a bug in fMRI software, which could invalidate the results of a huge amount of research.

However, even being aware of the lack of 100% guarantee and certainty, modern neuroscience is potentially allowing us to demonstrate and even reinforce and prove so many things we suspected or intuitively knew about our brains. Thanks to this, modern technology plus the neuroscientists themselves dedicating their life's work are bringing us to a deeper understanding of ourselves. We can now truly understand that the more we as educators, trainers or coaches can bring this knowledge of the brain to our learners, the more effective their learning process is going to be. In fact, I personally believe we are well under way in an era of neuroeducation, where our comprehension of the brain is key to more effective and efficient learning processes. Also, I believe that a deeper comprehension will lead to humanity communicating together in a totally different way and developing new ways of living and moving forward through the twenty-first century.

Additionally, we are living in times with big question marks relating to education in general, and certainly there are great advances regarding the introduction of emotional intelligence in schools, as well as the belief of new practices, such as the introduction of meditation for children. The educational systems seem to follow a one-size-fits-all approach that does not respect what we now know about the brain: that each brain is unique and different to any other brain. Additionally, teachers are overloaded with administration and bureaucracy and tend to have less and less time for the more humane side of teaching – that is, the necessary human contact and deeper empathetic connection with the learner.

---

[3] Eklund, A., Nichols, T.E., and Knutsson, H. (2016) *Cluster failure: Why fMRI inferences for spatial extent have inflated false positive rates'*. PNAS 113(28), 7900–7905.

When the CEO of Tesla, Elon Musk, has taken his children out of mainstream education and created his own school for them, it makes me reflect. In an interview with Beijing TV in April 2015, Musk said that his school 'does away with the traditional great structure of American primary education'. His goal in the new school seems to be to cater for the skills of learners rather than force them to follow a set curriculum. I have also heard of many cases of children being taken out of school and given home tutoring and in most cases this has given excellent results with children flourishing far more than they ever did at school.

So, the real question for all of us nowadays is how we can adapt and improve how we learn. Definitely, those of us who are adopting new ways and new styles of delivery of teaching are recognising how our learners react differently. Through my desire to catalyse change to enhance our lives and in turn understanding the importance of education and in particular of language learning in a globalised world, I have taken the experience and learning about my own brain and I have researched so much of the amazing information that we now have access to. There is a wealth of information now: key facts about the brain; how to change our brains; how to have healthy brains and even how to maximise and optimise the performance of our brains, as well as amazing research and studies that continuously bring us new information. There are endless scientific reports and articles made available to us relating to neuroscientific research, and some interesting books relating to neuroscience and the brain. And neuroscience is pervading other areas of life, such as neuroeconomics, neuromarketing, neuroculture, neurolaw and neuroleadership to name just a few.

Most importantly, as I already mentioned, there is the question of neuroeducation and neurolearning, and we are shifting into an era where we begin to see how understanding our brains actually serves to optimise the learning process. There are many schools adopting this approach, as well as educational foundations that are also introducing social and emotional learning skills. In particular, there is the Hawn Foundation, founded by Goldie Hawn, which trains educators and children using MindUP™ – their signature programme which uses a brain-centric approach based on cognitive neuroscience, positive psychology and mindful awareness training. Ms. Hawn herself talks about how she has 'always been fascinated by the limitless potential of the brain and how she has seen first-hand the positive impact heart mind centric education has for children and educators'.[4] This positive impact is exactly what I have seen when people learn through the Neurolanguage Coaching approach, and all the certified Neurolanguage coaches worldwide are now witnessing this too.

In this book, I explain how Neurolanguage Coaching came about, what it consists of and also partly how it is delivered and how a coachee can learn from this process. The phenomena of language coaching, (in particular Neurolanguage Coaching) is storming the market because many language learners are now looking for something different and many corporates/businesses understand that their employees definitely need a degree of English that will allow them to conduct business on a global scale. Today, more and more businesses are working globally and cross-border and more and more people need language skills that are adequate for business. This means that people need a potentially faster, tailor-made and more efficient way of learning languages and especially to learn in a way that is adapted to their business. Neurolanguage Coaching can provide this new adapted learning style. In fact, Neurolanguage Coaching can assist private individuals as well as children who are learning languages.

In the first part of this book, we will take a look at some of the landmarks in the development of language teaching and also the current status of the language market, commenting on the types of teachers, trainers and coaches working with languages.

In the second part, we will talk about the development of neuroscience and the new era of neuroeducation, as well as introducing the underlying principles of neuroscience that are ever-pervasive in Neurolanguage Coaching.

---

[4] From *A Message from Goldie*, a now-retired page of Mind Up's website (accessed May 2016). For further information about the work of MindUp, see www.mindup.org.

Then, in the third part, we will move into coaching and language coaching/Neurolanguage Coaching. We will explore the differences between traditional language teaching and language coaching, as well as commenting on what Neurolanguage Coaching is not!

In the fourth part, we will go into the process and structure of Neurolanguage Coaching, examining the theoretical spiral learning process, the essential conversations and the structure and form of an engagement.

In part five, I will explain how to deliver grammar through brain-friendly coaching conversations, so that grammar becomes more pleasurable and fun to learn, as well as instantly graspable and applicable by the learner.

Finally, I will offer my thoughts on the way forward.

As a reader, I hope to inspire you to start an inward journey into your own brains and how to learn languages, encouraging and empowering you to know that we are all capable; it all depends on how we put our *mind* to the task.

If you are an educator, I hope to inspire you to initiate a deeper comprehension of how your own brain works to then transmit this information to your learner, giving you more insight into how to continually encourage, motivate and empower him/her.

The following quotes highlight the eternal task of the Neurolanguage coach:

> 'Tell me and I forget, teach me and I may remember, involve me and I learn.'
> — Benjamin Franklin

> 'I am not a teacher, but an awakener.'
> — Robert Frost

> 'The mediocre teacher tells. The good teacher explains. The superior teacher demonstrates. The great teacher inspires.'
> — William Arthur Ward

In the end, language is about communication, and the more we can communicate with each other on a worldwide basis, the more we will be able to understand, appreciate and respect each other.

> 'Communication leads to community, that is, to understanding, intimacy and mutual valuing.'
>
> – Rollo May

Part I

Today's language market – a thriving business worldwide

Nowadays, language acquisition could be regarded as imperative. In such a globalised world, English is definitely regarded as the major language, in particular for business. However, other languages have significant relevance and importance in different regions of the world. In particular, Mandarin is spoken by approximately 900 million native speakers and Spanish by 472 million native speakers in comparison to English, which is spoken by 339 million native speakers. However, English, as a native language and a second language, is in fact spoken by approximately 942 million people.[5]

Obviously, language learning is central to educational systems worldwide and language naturally forms a part of a school's curriculum. Private individuals also may wish to increase their foreign language knowledge for personal reasons. However, global business, wider geographical trade areas and, in addition, sophisticated modern technology all require the ability not only to converse in foreign languages but also to master foreign languages to such a degree that business success may be guaranteed. Indeed, most companies today know that they are fighting within international arenas and expect their top executives and leaders to have a certain command over languages, in particular the English language. Interestingly, Jean-Paul Nerriére presents 'Globish' as a common-ground language that non-native English speakers adopt in the context of international business.[6]

One of the major challenges today is how to motivate children within the educational systems to learn more languages and how to inspire children to want to learn. It is also interesting to note that many adult

---

[5] *Summary by Language Size*. Ethnologue database, 2015 edition. Dallas: SIL International.
[6] Nerrière, J.P., and Hon, D. (2009) *Globish the World Over: Volume 1*. St-Romain-en-Viennois: International Globish Institute.

learners of language were greatly impacted, often negatively, by the language learning process in their childhood and this, in fact, greatly affects their mindset regarding the learning process as an adult in business. Constant exposure to the target language is absolutely imperative for the brain to become accustomed to doing business in a foreign language.

When we look at the language teaching industry, there is a full array of different types of language teachers. This ranges from school teachers within the educational systems to qualified and non-qualified language teachers working privately or in the field of business. In fact, in the field of business it ranges from the famous backpacker who dabbles with language classes for some extra cash to the extremely qualified and/or extremely experienced language trainer who, in addition, possesses qualifications in a certain profession. For example, a qualified lawyer who delivers legal language training. One of the major questions in these cases is how to distinguish the quality and the experience of the trainer who is delivering such a service.

Over the last 15 years the phenomena of language coaching started to be heard – in particular, in connection with business language teaching services. Many business English teachers do, in fact, call themselves language coaches to distinguish themselves from other language teachers. The question as to what language coaching really is has become louder, and so the creation of the Neurolanguage Coaching approach and certification course[7] enables language teachers to certify as 'recognised language coaches', thus serving as a benchmark for the market to recognise those qualified and/or extremely experienced language trainers. Such trainers also possess a coaching accreditation as well as knowledge and insights regarding the principles of neuroscience and how the brain likes to learn. Actually, the language trainer who becomes a certified and accredited Neurolanguage coach not only possesses the necessary language expertise and accumulated teaching experience but also a much more brain-friendly coaching style that is adapted as much as possible to the learner.

---

[7] ELC Language Coaching Certification® – see www.languagecoachingcertification.com.

One of the major contradictions regarding language in the business world today is that companies expect so much language expertise from their employees and often support an in-house language learning programme. However, companies are continuously cost-cutting and often find themselves subsidising language learning and yet not achieving the required learning impact. Of course, this becomes the eternal dichotomy. Companies must cut costs and at the same time ensure quality learning that is effective and gives the company the necessary results for an effective globalised business. In this respect, it is recommended that companies really check the qualifications of the language trainer, teacher or coach. There should be proven language expertise, either through a language teaching qualification or proven years of experience. If a language coach is sought, ensure that there is in fact a coaching qualification and even go one step further and engage a Neurolanguage coach, who has the training as a coach as well as the training as a 'neuroeducator'. In addition, there should be active engagement in measuring the progress and success of the language learning – not only through testing, but also through regular goal-setting programmes with regular reviews of those goals. Employees mostly struggle with the fluency of spoken language, so there must be great emphasis on assisting employees to feel more comfortable and at ease when dealing in the target language. It may be that quality training and coaching costs more, but in the long run less time will be needed for the learning. So, effectively, in the long run, the company will in fact be paying less!

As an additional comment, companies should now bear in mind that no two brains are the same, so pushing people into large groups will not only produce low effective learning, but potentially harms some of those learners by causing increased embarrassment and discomfort when speaking the language. This means that a learner could potentially enter into panic mode with the language and could then suffer functional blockages in the two essential parts of the brain which have to be engaged for effective learning – the hippocampus and the prefrontal cortex – causing a detrimental effect and leading to difficulty in the application of the target language.[8] (We will be looking at this in more depth in the next part of this book.) Obviously, this would lead to a negative impact for the business.

[8] (a) Sandi, C., Pinelo-Nava, M. T. (2007) *Stress and memory: Behavioral effects and neurobiological mechanisms* Neural Plasticity 2007, e78970.
(b) Phelps, E. A. (2006) *Emotion and cognition: Insights from studies of the human amygdala.* Annual Review of Psychology 57, pp. 27–53.
(c) Arnsten, A. F. T. (1998) *Enhanced: The biology of being frazzled.* Science 280(5370), 1711–1712.

Key developments in English language teaching

If we just take a moment to look back in time and highlight some key moments in English language teaching,[9] we can see that only last century did language teaching begin to emerge as a discipline and profession. I will also endeavour to connect to key points that link with the concept of Neurolanguage Coaching.

English language teaching actually started back in 1946, when the British Council took the decision to sponsor a journal called *English Language Teaching (ELT)*. As such, the profession was born and with it teacher training and development. English language teaching qualifications began in 1948, when a Chair at the Institute of Education at London University was created.

From the 1950s to now, many different methods and approaches have been developed. The Association of Recognised English Language Schools (ARELS) was created in 1960 as a formal self-regulatory body, and later in 1967 the Association of Teachers of English as a Foreign Language (ATEFL) came into being and was internationalised as the IATEFL in 1971. In the US, the professional association called TESOL (Teaching English to Speakers of Other Languages) was established in 1966.

During the 1960s and 1970s, both ELT and applied linguistics flourished. In the 1960s, A. S. Hornby began teaching language in 'situations' and 'actions', creating the situational approach. Other methods also developed, such as the natural method or direct method.

---

[9] For a deeper history of English language teaching, please refer to Howatt, A.P.R., with Widdowson, H.G. (2004) *A History of English Language Teaching ELT*, 2nd ed. Oxford: Oxford University Press.

Interestingly from the Neurolanguage Coaching perspective, in the 1970s the 'communicative approach' (communicative language teaching – CLT) developed. It is based upon considering the way language works in real life, how we apply language and how we should take this into account when teaching languages. I definitely would say that Neurolanguage Coaching follows on from this approach, with the added dimensions of the coaching approach and the brain-friendly conversations derived from the practical application of the principles of neuroscience. As with Neurolanguage Coaching, the communicative approach was mainly for adult learners and moved more towards specific needs learning, and this opened the doors for English for Specific Purposes (ESP). At that time there was quite a demand for ESP, which grew more and more, and throughout the 1970s both ELT and ESP continued to develop.

By the late 1970s some believed that ELT was 'too technical and remote from the human concerns of teachers as well as learners'.[10] Earl W. Stevick published articles and books between 1976 and 1990 to try and bring back 'humanistic methods' into language teaching.

Nowadays, globalisation and computerisation have had, and continue to have, a great influence on ELT. In addition, there is a question relating to the need for social interaction as opposed to computerised interaction. From neuroscientific research such as Lieberman's work, we know that 'being socially connected is our brain's lifelong passion',[11] and Lieberman continues by stating that research suggests that we are more likely to remember information when we take it in socially. In addition, we know that to learn effectively the brain needs real and personal interaction, generating and sharing information with others.[12] (Obviously, this is key to the argument that computerised learning will never have the same efficiency and effect as human interaction. From the Neurolanguage Coaching perspective, I would

---

[10] *Ibid.*, p. 255

[11] Lieberman, M. D. (2013) *Social: Why our brains are wired to connect.* Oxford: Oxford University Press.

[12] Davachi, L., Kiefer, T., Rock, D., and Rock, L. (2010) *Learning that lasts through AGES.* NeuroLeadership Journal 3, pp. 53–63.

always advocate the need for the human interaction with the possible additional backup of computerised programmes.)

Let us now take another step back in time and take a look at some of the other methods prior to the communicative approach such as the natural method (Sauveur) and the direct method (Berlitz) and start to connect these with today.

I heartily concur with what John Locke[13] wrote in 1693:

> Men learn languages for the ordinary intercourse of Society and Communication of thoughts in common Life without any farther design in the use of them. And for this purpose, the Original way of Learning a Language by Conversation, not only serves well enough but is to be prefer d as the most Expedite, Proper and Natural.

The natural method was developed by Lambert Sauveur in the late 1870s and in his work *An Introduction to the Teaching of Living Languages without Grammar or Dictionary*,[14] I really like the way he gave his invaluable advice on how to talk to learners. He said that there are two basic principles. The first was only to ask 'earnest questions' and the second was 'to connect scrupulously the questions in such a manner that one may give rise to another'. When I reflect upon this, I do believe that one of the strong elements of Neurolanguage Coaching is the constant powerful provocative questions that indeed provoke the learner to encode the new language information in the area of the brain that governs memory encoding.

In the latter part of the nineteenth century, the direct method emerged. The story tells us that Berlitz,[15] who was an immigrant in the USA, was working as a language teacher at a college. He became ill and was substituted by Nicholas Joly, who took Mr. Berlitz's French class. In

---

[13] From John Locke's open letter titled *Some Thoughts Concerning Education*, now widely available online.

[14] Sauveur, L. (1875) *An Introduction to the Teaching of Living Languages without Grammar or Dictionary*, quoted in Howatt, A.P.R., with Widdowson, H.G. (2004) *A History of English Language Teaching ELT*, 2nd ed. Oxford: Oxford University Press, pp. 218 –21.

[15] The Berlitz Corporation operates worldwide as language instruction, translation and localisation services.

fact, Joly could not speak a word of English, so he delivered the lessons only in French for the six weeks that Mr. Berlitz was ill. When Berlitz returned, he was astounded that his students were speaking French quite well, with good pronunciation and grammar. This inspired him to create the Berlitz Method, or direct method, with the philosophy that learners from the first moment on should be exposed only to the target language. However, this is in fact a point on which Neurolanguage Coaching differs from the Berlitz Method. Firstly, as we will see from the neuroscience part of this book, speaking to and teaching beginners with only the target language could negatively impact and deeply affect the emotional brain of the learner. We will see how this impact could in fact hinder and block the learning process.

Secondly, as will be seen later in this book, I am a firm believer in learning by association, and the more that the learner's brain can associate and make connections between the native language and the target language, the faster the learning process seems, and the higher the chance of the information being remembered. On the other hand, I am not saying that the native language should be continuously spoken. Not at all! I strongly believe that accustoming the brain to the target language and constantly exposing the brain to the target language is extremely beneficial and aids the learning process. What I am saying is that there should be the freedom to use the native language and also to explain whenever necessary in the native language, so that the emotional brain remains calm and 'normalised'.

Neurolanguage Coaching is based on a flow of interactive conversation to get the learner into what is known as the 'performing brain' and in addition the provocative questions of the coach should continuously be provoking 'brain connections' regarding the target language. In this way, Neurolanguage Coaching reflects Locke s observation that conversation is key, and Sauveur's remarks concerning 'earnest' questions.

As another contrasting example of native vs target language, Harold E. Palmer, who developed the oral method in the 1920s, also excluded

---

16 Palmer, H. E. (1921) *The Principles of Language-Study*. New York: World Book Company.

teaching grammar in the students' native language because he believed that grammatical rules should come through 'habit formation'.[16] Here I strongly believe and, in fact, have personally witnessed that the more we can help our learner to connect to existing language knowledge and structures, the faster they will learn the target language. This doesn't mean we have to deliver grammar in native language: we can also deliver through the target language, level permitting, but we can constantly ask our learners to reflect upon the similarities or dissimilarities of the grammar with known native structures. Interestingly, recent research led by Kirsten Weber at the Max Planck Institute in Nijmegen tells us: 'Processing a known structure is easier for the brain second time round. As a whole, our study shows that we seem to use the same brain areas for native and new language structures and that "Alienese" was in the process of being integrated into the participants' existing language brain networks.'[17]

Stephen Krashen and Tracy Terrell developed the natural approach method of language teaching, the theoretical aspects of which were published in their book *The Natural Approach* in 1983.[18] This approach actually shares a lot with the direct method practised by Sauveur, Berlitz and others and also focused on the idea of enabling natural language acquisition as well as developing communicative skills. I do believe that Krashen's hypothesis, regarding the acquisition learning hypothesis and the affective filter hypothesis, reflect how the brain learns and how the brain is affected by distress or social pain. I talk more about this in Part II, which discusses neuroscience and Neurolanguage Coaching.

Another later development relating to the communicative approach was the Dogme language teaching movement which came about in the mid-1990s and aims to focus language teaching on real conversations about real subjects. As I already mentioned, this is what Neurolanguage

---

[17] Weber, K., Christiansen, M.K., Magnus Petersson, K.M., Indefrey, P., and Hagoort, P. (2016) *fMRI syntactic and lexical repetition effects reveal the initial stages of learning a new language.* Journal of Neuroscience 36, 6872–6880.

[18] Krashen, S., and Terrell, T. (1983) *The Natural Approach: Language Acquisition in the Classroom.* Oxford: Pergamon Press.

Coaching believes in, and we know that the brain prefers real and personal relevance to the learner which, in turn, enhances the learning capacity.

If we really looked deeply into the development of language learning throughout the last century, we could witness a constant push and pull between the traditional methods such as grammar translation and the more progressive methods such as the communicative approach. In addition, as in all disciplines, some methods or approaches were more in favour at a given time due to the influential parties steering such trends. Now, I would suggest, as we move further into the twenty-first century, the question is how to integrate all the wisdom gained from the past to enable and facilitate, wherever possible, a faster and more efficient learning process which is, in turn, necessary for a global world and global business. Additionally, such a learning process should follow the principles that we now know concerning how the brain functions, connects and learns and – most importantly – respecting the fact that every brain is unique.

As a final note to this part, Howatt and Widdowson[19] talk about learning a language through constant conversation. They state that 'learning how to speak a new language, it is held, is not a rational process which can be organised in a step-by-step manner following graded syllabuses of new points to learn, exercises and explanations. It is an intuitive process for which human beings have a natural capacity that can be awakened provided only that the proper conditions exist.'

And this awakening is exactly what Neurolanguage Coaching aspires to do.

---

[19] Howatt, A.P.R., with Widdowson, H.G. (2004) *A History of English Language Teaching ELT*, 2nd ed. Oxford: Oxford University Press, p. 210.

Part II

The new era of neuroscience

In this new era of neuroscience, people like me, who are not neuroscientists, are able to start to understand the amazing potential within us: the brain. I might add, though, that it is not only about understanding our brain, but also potentially understanding the holistic functioning of brain, heart and gut in unison. (Interestingly, yesterday I was reading that scientists are now connecting Parkinson's disease with gut bacteria!)[20]

This part of the book gives readers a simplified understanding of the areas of neuroscientific research that are relevant to the question of how the learning process is affected or enhanced, and particularly the role that this plays in Neurolanguage Coaching. It may be a very superficial view of the whole topic of neuroscience. In fact, I do not go into great detail, as I believe it is 'the coming together' of various aspects that presents the key to a holistic brain approach. So, at first I take you through a basic understanding, which then leads to the hypothesis that there are various principles that influence our approach and lead to a 'perfect learning state' in my interpretation. After this, I have focused in on the seven key principles as the 'underlying neuroscientific principles'.

Neuroscience is the study of how the nervous system develops as well as its structure and what it does. Many researchers say that neuroscience is the same as neurobiology; however, the latter looks at the biology of the nervous system whereas neuroscience looks at anything to do with the nervous system. From the 1950s onwards, neuroscience started to make significant advances and over the last 25 years, new technology like fMRI scans (functional magnetic resonance

---

[20] Sampson, T.R., Debelius, J.W., Thron, T., Janssen, S., Shastri, G.G. *et al.* (2016) *Gut microbiota regulate motor deficits and neuroinflammation in a model of Parkinson's disease.* Cell 167(6), 1469–1480.

imaging) allow us to see 'the brain in action' and in certain research even structural changes to the brain.

Our brain primarily consists of nerve cells called neurons, but neurons are actually the most fundamental cells of our nervous system. The brain contains roughly one hundred billion nerve cells forming between a trillion to even quadrillion neural connections. Neurons do actually communicate directly with one another sending messages in the form of electrochemical signals or impulses, but neurons do not actually touch each other as there is always a space between them called a synapse. This gap, amazingly, is about 1 millionth of a centimetre wide (I never cease to be amazed whenever I try to imagine this). In very simple terms, cell-to-cell communication occurs when an action potential travels down a neuron to the synaptic gap to connect with other neurons or other cells. This is very nicely expressed by Hebb's Law, which states that 'cells that fire together wire together'.[21] Whenever there is brain activity, there can be millions of neurons firing together at the same time and this firing produces electrical activity, which can be measured or monitored by an electro-encephalography, or EEG for short. Multiple electrodes are placed along the scalp and the EEG measures the voltage fluctuations. Neurons connect to create incredibly vast and intricate neural networks. Our neural networks or maps are in fact our personal internal representations of the external world. Interestingly, wherever we focus our attention and energy, those brain maps will become more ingrained or embedded into long-term memory. However, just as an additional note and owing to my simplified overview, we shouldn't forget that there are in fact many other cells in the brain besides neurons that do indeed have important functions and which also make synapses.

I believe that one of the major breakthroughs we have had with regard to the past neuromyths about the brain is the realisation that the brain is in fact plastic and not static, meaning that the brain can remodel and

---

[21] Hebb, D.O. (1949) *The Organization of Behavior.* New York: Wiley & Sons.

remap its connections. Neuroplasticity is the ability of the brain and nervous system to change structurally and functionally in response to its experience. By learning new things and having new experiences, the brain starts to embed new patterns of neural networks, thus reshaping itself. There has been quite a lot of research relating to neuroplasticity, and some amazing results. For example, studies show after six to eight weeks of regular meditation the prefrontal cortex becomes thicker and the amygdala shrinks.[22] Meanwhile, London taxi drivers apparently have a developed area of spatial navigation in their hippocampus due to the years and years of 'mapping' the streets of London in their brains.[23]

Another amazing breakthrough happened in 1998 when scientists discovered, contrary to previous beliefs, the human brain produces new nerve cells into adulthood.[24] This gave us the clear evidence of neurogenesis, the creation of new neurons, thus breaking down the neuromyth that adults were not able to produce new brain cells. Now we know we do! In 2016, research is also demonstrating that after a certain period of aerobic exercise, the generation of neurons kicks in.[25] This neurogenesis is seen to 'occur' in the hippocampus, which is the brain structure important for learning.

[22] Taren, A.A., Creswell, D., and Gianaros, P.J. (2013) *Dispositional mindfulness co-varies with smaller amygdala and caudate volumes in community adults PLOS ONE* 8(5), e64571

[23] Maguire, E.A., Woollett, K., Spiers, H.J. *London taxi drivers and bus drivers: A structural MRI and neuropsychological analysis Hippocampus* 16(12), 1091–1101.

[24] Gage, F.H., and Kempermann, G. (1999) *New neural cells for the adult brain.* Scientific American 28(5), 48–53.

[25] Nokia, M.S., Lensu, S., Ahtiainen, J.P., Johansson, P.P., Koch, L.G. et al. (2016) *Physical exercise increases adult hippocampal neurogenesis in male rats provided it is aerobic and sustained* Journal of Physiology 594(7), 1855–1873.

With a basic understanding of:

➢ how neurons connect

➢ how the brain is plastic and can change and develop

➢ how neurogenesis is possible

we can encourage the change in mindset towards life-long learning and really encourage learners of any age. This is particularly necessary when a learner has a negative mindset towards learning at a later stage in life. We now **know** that we can learn and achieve the most amazing things at any age.

In addition, it is also essential to understand that every brain is different! Some scientists say that we genetically inherit about 50% of our neural networks and the other 50% consists of the input of our own knowledge and experiences throughout life. Others say only one third is genetic and two thirds are our own input. In any case, the amazing fact is that whatever I have as my genetic make-up plus all the knowledge that I possess in my brain is absolutely unique to me, just as your genetic make-up and whatever you have engrained in your brain – whether through learning, environmental exposure, life experience or whatever – is unique to you.

The crucial point to remember when we, as educators, are together with our learner or learners is:

➢ Each learner's brain is unique.

It is interesting and important to understand some of the key brain areas crucial to the learning process. Obviously, the brain in its entirety is important – metaphorically speaking, all instruments in an orchestra have a definite role – but there are some key areas which will afford a better understanding of Neurolanguage concepts.

The first area to highlight is the cerebellum, which plays an important role in motor control, and prior to the 1990s was believed to be purely motor-related. Research shows it is also active regarding language, attention and mental imagery.[26] Studies show that there are interactions between the cerebellum and other areas of the cerebral cortex, which is the outer covering of grey matter over the hemispheres. Now there is speculation on whether the cerebellum is also part of the unconscious mind which learns, remembers and stores actions and responses in particular from early childhood. It is where our subconscious patterns, repeated actions, habits, skills and even emotional reactions are stored.[27] The cerebellum contains more than half of all the neurons in the human brain.[28]

The next area to highlight is the hippocampus, which could be described as a memory 'organiser' and 'encoder'. It decides what should be stored in short-term memory and in long-term memory. It is also important for spatial navigation. Obviously, the hippocampus is essential for learning as it is the 'boss' for memory encoding in the brain.

The prefrontal cortex is the portion of the cerebral cortex which covers the front part of the frontal lobe of the brain. It carries out our 'executive function', meaning that it is our conscious thinking brain. Analysing, creating, planning, learning, remembering, making decisions and even visualising all take place in this part of the brain. It is the part that is the most active when we are consciously concentrating, and it is involved in working memory.

Finally, for our purposes, it is essential to mention the amygdala. The amygdala is part of the emotional brain or the limbic system and in simple terms could be described as responsible for triggering the alarm

[26] Marien, P., Ackermann, H., Adamszek, M., Barwood, C.H.S., Beaton, A. et al. (2014) *Consensus paper: Language and the cerebellum: an ongoing enigma*. Cerebellum 13(3), 386–410.

[27] Dispenza, J. (2007) *Evolve Your Brain: The Science of Changing Your Mind*. Deerfield Beach, FL: Health Communications Inc.

[28] Ibid.

whenever a survival question arises. It's fascinating to think, in fact, that a part of our brain is constantly scanning and checking that we are 'safe' and out of 'danger', and the amygdala forms part of the mechanism that immediately alerts the body to any threat situation. Interestingly, the amygdala will also create certain emotions like rage to protect us in life-threatening situations. In his book *Emotional Intelligence*,[29] Daniel Goleman also refers to the amygdala hijack, where our emotions can actually override the conscious brain, leading us to emotional reactions that we may not rationally understand. When the alarm sound is triggered, urgent messages are sent to every major part of the brain. The body's fight or flight[30] mechanisms start to mobilise. We all know those tell-tale signs of quickened heart rate, raised blood pressure, rapid breathing, shaking, blurred vision and unclear thoughts, which are all manifestations of the body in fight or flight. It is interesting to note at this point that the body preparing itself for this fight or flight directs blood away from the visceral organs of the body into the extremities – the arms and the legs – enabling either the 'stay and fight' scenario or the 'run away fast' scenario. This signifies that in those moments conscious and rational thought move to the 'back of the queue', because in this survival mode we really do not have the time to be hanging around analysing and debating if we should fight or run! So, the two major areas needed for the learning process, the prefrontal cortex and the hippocampus, are both affected.[31]

Nowadays, we are constantly exposed to situations that can be negatively perceived as a threat by our brain (such as delivering a presentation in a foreign language!). We also now know from research that when we experience social pain, our brain does in fact

---

[29] Goleman, D. (1995) *Emotional Intelligence*. London: Bloomsbury.

[30] First described in 1929 by Walter Bradford Cannon in *Bodily Changes in Pain, Hunger, Fear, and Rage*. New York: Appleton-Century-Crofts.

[31] (a) Sandi, C., Pinelo-Nava, M. T. (2007) *Stress and memory: Behavioral effects and neurobiological mechanisms* Neural Plasticity *2007*, e78970.
(b) Phelps, E.A. (2006) *Emotion and cognition: Insights from studies of the human amygdala*. Annual Review of Psychology 57, 27–53.
(c) Arnsten, A.F.T. (1998) *Enhanced: The biology of being frazzled*. Science 280(5370), 1711–1712.

activate neural regions that also activate when there is physical pain.[32] So, in effect, we could conclude from this that the brain registers social pain in the same area of the brain and to the same degree as it does when it registers physical pain. We know from what we mentioned above that life-threatening situations trigger the amygdala and 'limbic reactions', and we also know that social pain and emotional pain can also trigger the same reactions to a lesser or greater degree. A nice example of some 'amygdala arousers' can be understood in the SCARF® model by David Rock.[33] This model illustrates five domains of human social experience which could trigger the fight or flight response in a given situation.

Let us now imagine a scenario where speaking a foreign language triggers the brain into that feeling of being in a life-threatening situation. The survival mechanism kicks in and conscious rational thought processes no longer occur, with resources becoming limited to the executive functions of the prefrontal cortex and memory function of the hippocampus. In this way, the learner feels totally blocked and closed to the learning process, but in essence this block is actually real, due to those limited resources to the areas needed for learning. Indeed, learning a language could trigger all types of reactions: typically, shame and embarrassment as well as feelings of uncertainty, inadequacy, frustration and not being good enough. There is even the phenomena of foreign language anxiety, or xenoglossophobia,[34] which has been set into three main areas: communication apprehension, test anxiety and fear of negative evaluation. In any of the aforementioned cases, the brain could be triggered into social pain, which could then lead to negative limbic reactions.

[32] Eisenberger, N.I. (2012) *The neural bases of social pain: evidence the shared representations with physical pain* Psychosomatic Medicine 74(2), 126–135.

[33] SCARF is an acronym of the social concerns that drive human behaviour: status, certainty, autonomy, relatedness and fairness. See Rock, D. (2008) *SCARF: A brain-based model for collaborating with and influencing others.* Neuroleadership Journal 1(1), 44.

[34] Horwitz, E.K., Horwitz, M.B., Cope, J. (1896) *Foreign language classroom anxiety.* Modern Language Journal 70(2), 125–132.

So, the teacher, trainer and coach should be:

➢ fully able to understand the key roles of the cerebellum, hippocampus and prefrontal cortex in the learning process.

➢ fully aware of the amygdala and limbic system reactions to potential threat.

➢ fully empathetic to any type of social or emotional pain or foreign language anxiety in a learner, as this triggered reaction could impact and impede the learning process.

➢ fully able to coach the learner around the perceived threat situation, so that the brain can return to its normal calm and unthreatened state

Now, let us have a simplistic look at the learning process. From pre-birth to age seven, the brain is constantly absorbing brand new information and constantly making new neural connections. In particular, at this age we are forging subconscious programs that enable us to function and survive. For example, walking, talking, getting dressed, washing, etc. all become activities that we are able to perform without thinking. Obviously, a child's brain has amazing plasticity, capable of surprising achievements such as becoming bilingual at such early ages. Through studies, we now understand that the best age for children to learn languages is in fact between two and four years old.[35]

From the age of six, our brains seemingly shift from predominant subconscious mind into a 'calm consciousness',[36] and it could be said that we initiate the development of 'the conscious brain'. Between the

---

[35] O Muircheartaigh, J., Dean, D.C., Dirks, H., Waskiewicz, N., Lehman, K. et al. (2013) *Interactions between white matter asymmetry and language during neurodevelopment.* Journal of Neuroscience 33(41), 16170–16177.

[36] Taken from chapter 1 of Lipton, B., and Bhaerman, S. (2010) *Spontaneous Revolution: Our Positive Future and a Way to Get There From Here.* London: Hay House.

ages of six and twelve, 'children's neurons grow more and more synapses that serve as new pathways for nerve signals'.[37]

This also means that the learning process begins to change, and whereas previously the brain was absorbing information and creating subconscious programs, from now on the conscious brain develops and we move from 'subconscious absorption' to learning through association. This means that the brain starts to take in new information and tries to relate it to existing information that is already stored in our brains. In other words, our brain tries to connect the new with past experience. This is especially relevant in the process of target language acquisition, as according to this associative learning process there should be a constant attempt to 'associate', wherever possible, target language with native language, and on the contrary to 'disassociate' whenever it leads to something misleading and gives rise to a false friend. As I mentioned before, we start to have more hints of this from neuroscience and recent research (2016), led by Kirsten Weber at the Max Planck Institute Nijmegen. The study tells us: 'Processing a known structure is easier for the brain second time round. As a whole, our study shows that we seem to use the same brain areas for native and new language structures.'[38]

> So, as a language educator we should be able:
>
> ➢ to constantly stimulate the learning process through provocative association (whenever possible) of native language and target language.

One interesting question is whether the 'perfect learning state' for the brain actually exists, and I would really like to explore this question.

---

[37] Willis, J. (2006) *Research-based Strategies to Ignite Student Learning.* Alexandria, VA: ASCD.
[38] Weber, K., Christiansen, M.K., Magnus Petersson, K.M., Indefrey, P., and Hagoort, P. (2016) *fMRI syntactic and lexical repetition effects reveal the initial stages of learning a new language.* Journal of Neuroscience 36, 6872–6880.

Recent findings about memory formation have been summarised by a model called AGES[39] – Attention, Generation, Emotion and Spacing. The model's creators write: 'With just the right amount of these variables, learners intensively activate their hippocampus, which creates deep circuits for easy retrieval.' This would hint towards a perfect learning state. However, I personally believe that two additional elements should be considered and would strongly recommend adding Intention and Motivation to create the IMAGES model, representing the complete ingredients which are key to maximising learning and the indication of moving towards the perfect learning state.

Intention is obviously a necessary ingredient, as without the intention to do something we just would not do it. Additionally, motivation is a critical component of learning. People who are motivated to learn something use higher cognitive processes when learning. These two elements can be seen as interconnected, because I may have the intention to do something but I may not be motivated to do it. (May I add the personal example of my strong intention to go running every day, but, believe me, with no motivation to do so!) Conversely, I may have the motivation to do something, but not intend to do it anyway.

> So, IMAGES means:
>
> ➢ enough Intention, Motivation, Attention, Generation, Emotions and Spacing may form the components comprising a 'perfect learning state'.

Together with this concept, I do believe there is also a need to reflect on the ideal brainwaves which should be predominant during 'this so-called perfect learning state'. As we previously mentioned above, when masses of neurons communicate with each other synchronised electrical pulses are generated, producing brainwaves. According to what we are doing or feeling, our brainwaves change. Frequency is measured in hertz. As I mentioned previously, brainwaves are monitored and measured by an EEG.

---

[39] Davachi, L., Kiefer, T., Rock, D., and Rock, L. (2010) *Learning that lasts through AGES*. Neuroleadership Journal 3, 53–63.

Here is a simplified[40] overview to explain the different brainwaves:

- Delta waves are dominant when we are in deepest meditation or dreamless sleep.
- Theta waves also occur during sleep and in deep meditation, and this state is where the gateway to our subconscious lies, thus the gateway to learning and memory.
- Alpha brainwaves are predominant when we go into a quiet, calm consciousness state. If we just take a moment to focus and concentrate on our breathing, the brain would begin to shift into alpha brainwaves. Alpha indicates a very calm resting state for the brain. In 2015, I had the pleasure of meeting Dr. James Hardt, one of the world s leading specialists in brainwaves and biofeedback,[41] Dr. Hardt commented to me that 'when the brain is in alpha, it is almost as if the alpha brainwaves massage the limbic system'. From his comment, I understand that if the brain is in alpha, then the limbic system cannot become aroused. In his White Paper,[42] Jeffrey L. Fannin states that 'people who spend their time mostly in alpha brainwaves possess enhanced memory, with the ability to learn new skills and potentially genius-like abilities'.
- Beta brainwaves predominate when we are attentive, making decisions or involved in focus mental activity. Beta brainwaves are divided into three bands: firstly, low beta, when we are pondering over something; second, mid beta, when we are actively thinking about something; and high beta when we are really undergoing complex thought or experiencing high anxiety or excitement. Obviously, when we are about to sit an exam we can expect to be experiencing mid and high beta

---

[40] There are other brainwaves, in particular gamma brainwaves, but I do not talk about these here. Even though I believe gamma waves are a subject of extreme interest, they're probably better discussed in another book!

[41] More information on Dr. James V. Hardt can be found on the Biocybernaut Institute's website, www.biocybernaut.com/partners.

[42] Fannin, J.L. [no date] *Understanding Your Brainwaves (white paper)*. See www.drjoedispenza.com/files/understanding-brainwaves_white_paper.pdf.

brainwaves. Too much beta activity, and especially too much over prolonged periods of time, is negative, leading to stress, anxiety, muscle tension and even insomnia and addiction.[43]

If we speculate for a moment, we could actually think about connecting our potentially perfect learning state together with the perfect brainwave activity, to give us the ideal scenario for learning effectively and efficiently; this means the brain would be dancing from predominance of mid-beta to low beta to predominant alpha brainwaves. Mid beta would occur when we are working something out, so highly engaging brain activity; then low beta would manifest when we are pondering or musing on the information; and then alpha would indicate the more reflective integration of the learning.

> All in all, I would suggest that as a neuroeducator we should:
>
> ➢ constantly aim for a learner to be in a continuous state of calm and tranquillity together with positive emotions and generating the appropriate brainwaves to reflect this state, ideally oscillating constantly between mid-beta to alpha.

We also need to reflect upon the continuous interplay in our minds between the conscious and the subconscious brain. In his book *The Inner Game of Tennis*,[44] Timothy Gallwey writes about what he calls the thinking brain and the performing brain and how the thinking brain often interferes and hinders the performing brain. In terms of language learning, we know that native tongue interference can affect acquisition and fluency of a target language, and when we are able to

---

[43] For more about brainwaves, see Dispenza, J. (2007) *Evolve Your Brain: The Science of Changing Your Mind*. Deerfield Beach, FL: Health Communications Inc.

[44] Gallwey, W.T. (1997) *The Inner Game of Tennis: The Classic Guide to the Mental Side of Peak Performance*. New York: Random House.

quieten that native language interference, the performing brain may take over and fluency may flourish.

In this way, I would also suggest that it is always necessary for the neuroeducator:

> to get the learner into a state where the subconscious mind is the main performer and the conscious mind takes a back seat.

So, just reflecting on all I have mentioned regarding the different aspects of neuroscience, are we in a new era of neuroeducation?

I truly believe that the answer is YES. We are gaining more insights into how our brains react and function and how we learn and, yes, there appears to be a moving trend in which emotional intelligence and principles of neuroscience are penetrating the learning process, and I strongly believe that we are now in a new educational era: the era of neuroeducation.

25 years ago, the field of neuroeducation started to create whispers in the academic world, concretely in 1988 by the formation of the Psychophysiology and Education Special Interest Group. It is now the cornerstone of many research organisations around the world, and educational neuroscience, or neuroeducation,[45] has not only emerged from the whispers but is now fully underway in practice as evidenced by various people who are marrying neuroscience with education of some type or other.

According to Aalok Mehta, neuroeducation 'is an interdisciplinary field that combines neuroscience, psychology and education to create improved teaching methods and curricula and is moving increasingly close to prime time, as researchers gain a more sophisticated

---

[45] Mehta, A. (2009). *Neuroeducation emerges as insights into brain development, learning abilities grow.* Published online at The Dana Foundation, NY, USA. Available at: http://www.dana.org/Publications/Brainwork/Details.aspx?id=43782.

understanding of how young minds develop and learn, leading education and brain experts say.'[46]

In reality, neuroscience is seemingly penetrating all walks of life nowadays: education, leadership and executive development, health, even spirituality and law! (Neuroleadership, neuroeconomics, neurolaw, etc!)

Focusing in on neuroeducation, the more we are discovering about how the brain works, the more we are able to bring this comprehension into educational methods and approaches, to create brain-friendly conversations and ultimately brain-friendly learning. And that is exactly the philosophy upon which I created the concept of Neurolanguage Coaching.

Based on the knowledge we now have regarding the brain and how the brain likes to learn, we are blasting away those 'neuromyths'[47] that have hindered and disempowered for far too long and we are now tapping into and encouraging more and more learning potential, due to the fact that as neuroeducators we now know HOW to. Pettito and Dunbar stated that educational neuroscience 'provides the most relevant level of analysis for resolving today's core problems in education'.[48] According to Frith, 'Learning in cognitive psychology and neuroscience has focused on how individual humans and other species have evolved to extract useful information from the natural and social worlds around them.'[49]

Neuroscience is providing new information regarding the current state of a learner that could be especially relevant to learning and teaching.

---

[46] Ibid.

[47] della Chiesa, B., et al. (eds.) (2007) *Understanding the Brain: Towards a New Learning Science.* Paris: OECD.

[48] Petitto, L. A., and Dunbar, K. (2004) *New findings from educational neuroscience on bilingual brains, scientific brains, and the educated mind.* Paper presented at the Conference on Usable Knowledge in Mind, Brain and Education, Cambridge, MA. In Fischer, K., and Katzir, T. (eds.) *Building Usable Knowledge in Mind, Brain, & Education.* Cambridge: Cambridge University Press.

[49] Frith, C. (2007). *Making Up the Mind: How the Brain Creates Our Mental World.* Oxford: Blackwell.

The possibility to now have insights into brain states, genetic states and hormonal states, as well as brain structure and activity, will really enable us to ascertain the best ways of delivering and learning. One example of this is the research which shows us that we can distinguish between learning mathematics by rote or learning through conceptual understandings.[50]

At this point, I would like to suggest that the key is actually in the 'neuroeducators' themselves. I truly believe that once we teachers, trainers, coaches are able to fully understand and embrace the findings that modern neuroscience is enlightening us with – and not only understand and embrace but actually put this knowledge into practice daily with all of our learners and students – we then create brain-friendly education. We would be much more aware of the impact that we as teachers, trainers, instructors or coaches actually have on the learner. This is something that over the past two years I personally, and nearly all those who have certified with me as Neurolanguage coaches, have witnessed in learners. Neuroeducators are bridging the education–neuroscience gap by bringing neuroscience alive in a practical sense and not only in theory. Ultimately, the greatest transformation is us as neuroeducators, as we are the ones who are able to really empower the learner throughout the learning process.

Over the last year, I have worked with language teachers all over the world, training and certifying them to become Neurolanguage coaches. I have witnessed teachers absolutely transform and metamorphose with their newly acquired knowledge of the brain, neural connections and neuroplasticity. I have seen how they really assist the learner to be empowered to learn and come into his/her own full potential. In our case of language learning, this knowledge, together with the incorporation of a coaching style, coaching principles and competencies, notably enhances and potentially utterly transforms the language learning process.

---

[50] Ischebeck, A., Zamarian, L., Siedentopf, C., Koppelstäatter, F., Benke, T., et al. (2013) *How specifically do we learn? Imaging the learning of multiplication and subtraction.* Neuroimage 30(4), 1365–1375.

In the study by Dimitris Zeppos titled 'Profiling Neurolanguage coaches Worldwide',[51] one of the major findings has been that most of the people who have certified as language coaches are highly qualified middle-aged teachers, who, at such an age, are people that want to change and make a difference to the world. This is, in fact, very much the feeling that is resonating in all upcoming branches of neuroeducation – the need to make a difference and bring education forward into the twenty-first century. In particular, Neurolanguage Coaching has the mission to bring foreign language learning into the twenty-first century, facilitating more and more multi-lingual communication in an ever more globalised world.

As a summary, I would like to repeat the highlighted bullets which comprise the holistic contribution from the neuroscientific principles, which the neuroeducator comprehends and ultimately conveys:

➢ how neurons connect.

➢ how the brain is plastic and can change and develop.

➢ how neurogenesis is possible.

➢ that each learner's brain is unique.

➢ the key roles of the cerebellum, hippocampus and prefrontal cortex in the learning process.

➢ the important role of the amygdala and the absolute significance of limbic system reactions to perceived threat situations.

➢ that any type of social or emotional pain or foreign language anxiety in a learner is key, as this triggered reaction could impact and impede the learning process.

➢ how to coach the learner around the perceived threat situation, so that the brain can return to its normal calm and unthreatened state.

---

[51] Zeppos, D. (2014) *Profiling neurolanguage coaches worldwide – a case study.* World Journal of Education 4(6), 26–41.

➤ how to constantly stimulate the learning process through provocative association (whenever possible) of native language and target language.

➤ that enough IMAGES – Intention, Motivation, Attention, Generation, Emotions and Spacing – may form the components comprising a 'perfect learning state'.

➤ how to constantly aim for the learner's brain to be in a continuous state of calm and tranquillity together with positive emotions and generating the appropriate brainwaves to reflect this state, ideally oscillating constantly between mid-beta to alpha.

➤ how to get the learner into a state where the subconscious mind is the main performer and the conscious mind takes a back seat.

The underlying principles of neuroscience pervasive in Neurolanguage Coaching

Drawing upon what I have just highlighted in the previous part about the brain and how the brain learns, Neurolanguage Coaching is about being constantly conscious of the underlying principles that will enable the learner to potentially have an optimal brain state for learning. Here are the **seven core principles** that are pervasive throughout Neurolanguage Coaching engagements.

1. Striving for the constantly calm brain state

As I have already mentioned, when and if our brain perceives a threat, whether real or only perceived as real by the brain, our survival mechanism may kick in. In a language learning environment, the threat trigger can very easily be switched on. For example, feelings of embarrassment, shame, frustration, not reaching perfection, feeling stupid or simply not wanting to speak can all lead to the fight or flight status. One such example that I would like to share with you is one particular client of mine who suffers extreme embarrassment relating to a strong mother tongue accent. This has affected my learner severely, and clearly this person has an emotional response when native English people comment or make fun of the accent. Over the past two years we have been consistently working to reduce this interference as well as build up this learner's confidence and also ability to defend himself, in particular with native English people who do not speak any second language (sadly it is normally those people who do not speak another language who criticise the most!). He and I have often discussed how the brain is reacting and the emotional triggers involved, and we have explored how he can deal with such situations. He has made excellent progress and is still striving to sound more and more native.

Now, I would like to give you an example from my own language learning experience. I can only describe the scenario as absolute terror to speak in Spanish. When I was 17 I moved to Spain to live. I had mastered written Spanish the two previous years, but could not speak it, but in only six months transformed my written knowledge into spoken and in the first few years there I became absolutely fluent with hardly any native accent interference. Most people thought I was Spanish!

When I was 20 I was given the opportunity to work in a small company, and even though I was confidently fluent by then and sounded native I suffered extreme fear and panic at the thought of answering the telephone. My colleagues thought it was funny, but I blatantly refused to pick up the phone whenever it rang! It took me six full months of courage to answer that phone. Looking back, I now understand that I was suffering from a threat response, which hindered and blocked me from behaving in a rational way and provoked 'telephone terror' in my brain.

This is just one example, and, as I mentioned before, emotional pain and social pain can essentially trigger limbic reactions,[52] which in turn can have a negative adverse effect on the two major regions of the brain – the prefrontal cortex and the hippocampus, which are areas essential to the learning process.

We can easily think of other scenarios in language learning situations which trigger emotional responses and that fight or flight response. Let me explore some of them.

Potential trigger: Uncertainty

The thought of learning any language could be so daunting that it might seem to be an impossible task. It could be that this thought triggers a threat response, as any language learning is in fact an

---

[52] See Dispenza, J. (2007) *Evolve Your Brain: The Science of Changing Your Mind.* Deerfield Beach, FL: Health Communications Inc., and Lieberman, M. D. (2013) *Social: Why our brains are wired to connect.* Oxford: Oxford University Press.

uncertain process per se. It could be seen as 'never-ending' and really not having an exact end point. If we think about our own native language, we never could honestly say that we utterly and completely know our own language. In this respect, learning a target language potentially triggers those feelings of it being an open and never-ending process. In other words, an immense feeling of uncertainty.

Calming the trigger

Neurolanguage Coaching endeavours to bring the necessary certainty into the process. From the outset, the process is clearly explained to the learner, and we help the learner to understand that the language will be built up step-by-step; essentially, we can say that we are going to be 'chunking the language down'. We conduct skilled coaching conversations that assist the learner to set their own goals, which are then worked on over a period of time until they are achieved. Once achieved, coach and coachee move on to a new goal-setting process to find the next 'chunks' to work on for another period of time. The learner feels in control of the process and the coach is the guide.

In addition, grammar-related topics are broken down and built up in a block-building process. This also brings more security and certainty and helps the learner feel in control. At all times, we want to keep the coachee calm and believing that he/she will learn the language in a systematically built up step-by-step fashion, and at all times we offer the necessary structure which allows the learner to feel constant achievement of goals, in other words a feeling of success and, consequently, the necessary motivation and inspiration to go further.

Potential trigger: Traditional teacher–student relationship

Another potential threat status trigger could arise from the traditional teacher–student scenario. Previously, teachers were often seen as the ultimate all knowledgeable experts with a superior status. Coaching hinges on the premise that both coach and coachee are on an equal status. Sometimes, though, a learner can feel inferior – less adequate.

Calming the trigger

The coach should be constantly acknowledging and giving positive feedback, so that the learner never feels inferior or intimidated. The flowing coaching conversations should allow the learner to feel safe to interact at any time and safe to express doubts, fears and questions.

Potential trigger – the coach feels threatened by the coachee

A situation may arise where, in a reverse of the above, the learner him/herself may feel that the coach is not adequate or not qualified enough to be coaching him/her, and this could even throw the coach into a threat response. I remember years ago arriving at my first appointment with a board member of an extremely big company group. This person came down to meet me at the reception of the company and then in the lift towered over me and stood far too close for comfort and proceeded to fire questions about me at me! I remember I calmly stood my ground. I did not move away and responded in a very quiet but firm manner. When I look back now, I understand that scenario as a potential vetting on behalf of my client, checking me out to see if I was good enough. I subsequently went on to work with this person for eight years, so I think I passed the test!

Calming the trigger

If there is a scenario in which the client really questions the qualification and capability of you, the coach, then one tactic is to strongly acknowledge the learner for his or her expertise and position; for example, 'You are the expert and, obviously, you know your specialised topic in your own language, and I am here to assist you to convert that knowledge into the target language, so in fact I'm here to be your sounding board to enable you to quickly transfer your expertise.'

Potential trigger: Group dynamics

Another potential threat trigger is the dynamic in group learning situations. The coach has to ensure that the group feels integrated and the coach should work on developing the feeling of working in a team, so that all the members of the group do not feel threatened by one another.

Calming the trigger

This can be achieved by introducing group goals, as well as group rules and desired behaviours. At all times, the coach should be empathetic with all group members and at the same time potentiate the group team dynamic.

Potential trigger: Independent learners

Sometimes a language coach may find that their learner is in fact an independent and quite solitary learner. Sir Winston Churchill famously said, 'I love to learn, but I do not want to be taught', and I have to confess that I am very much one of these people and I do not respond well to being given orders.

Calming the trigger

So, when faced with such a learner, the coach must be especially careful not to be giving orders or commands, as more often than not an independent learner will not appreciate being told what to do. In fact, to some people an order is an absolute 'turn-off'! The coach must adopt an extremely non-directive style, moving away from the traditional directive, demonstrative teaching style and adopting very calm coaching conversations that perfectly suit the independent learner. In addition, the language coach should be encouraging and supporting the learner to do as much as possible alone and again giving the feeling that the coach is his/her sounding board. Really finding out what an independent learner enjoys, likes or wants to do is also essential in this particular case.

Potential trigger: Forced to learn a language

A very common scenario nowadays is where employees in a company are forced to learn a new target language, which, in most cases, is English. I have in fact worked in various companies in Europe where the company language has been changed to English. In this scenario, the Neurolanguage coach is faced with learners who really do not want to be there and who do not want to learn. This can then trigger a lot of social pain feelings, which in turn lead to a non-optimal learning state.

Calming the trigger

In such a case, the coach should have an honest conversation from the beginning with the learner explaining how intention and motivation are absolutely essential for any learning process, and how without these the learning will just not be effective. Actually, acknowledging the social pain of the learner in this situation will be a first step to demonstrating empathy and an understanding of how the learner feels, which in turn will also help the learner to feel his/her views are appreciated. Often in this situation, there are strong feelings of an unfair situation and, certainly, when a company forces a language on an employee, it is indeed unfair!

Potential trigger: Xenoglossophobia

We have already touched upon foreign language anxiety or 'xenoglossophobia', which may be triggered from speaking, writing, reading or listening to a foreign language.[53]

Calming the trigger

One of the major missions of the Neurolanguage coach is to recognise any sign of a threat response and subsequent negative limbic response

---

[53] MacIntyre, P.D., Gardner, R.C. (1994) *The subtle effects of language anxiety on cognitive processing in the second language.* Language Learning 44(2), 283–305.

and be able to coach the learner around these. That way, the learner can return to a calm, normalised brain state once again, thus ensuring that optimal learning will take place. The brain also needs to experience real and personal situations, which are relevant to that individual person to make memories stick, as well as positivity, fun and enjoyment to ensure the flow of positive chemicals, in particular dopamine.[54] If the learner is really enjoying the process, as well as maintaining a constant calm brain state where the brain is oscillating between alpha and mid beta brainwaves (see my comment on the 'ideal brainwaves' in the previous part), then it is suggested that an optimal learning process can take place.

Here reference should be made again to Stephen Krashen's theory regarding the affective filter hypothesis.[55] Krashen's view is that when the affective filter is 'up' it impedes language acquisition and that 'affective variables' really do influence how the second language is acquired. So, negative feelings like low motivation, low self-esteem, and anxiety can 'raise' the affective filter and form a 'mental block', preventing the learning. Now we know from the perspective of social pain and threat status that indeed these 'blocks' or the scarcity of resources to the brain actually do physically occur.

> So, a constantly calm brain state is absolutely essential.

2. Motivation is absolutely crucial

Dr. Jeffrey Nevid writes: 'The term motivation refers to factors that activate, direct, and sustain goal-directed behavior ... Motives are the "whys" of behavior – the needs or wants that drive behavior and explain what we do. We don't actually observe a motive; rather, we infer that one exists based on the behavior we observe.'[56]

---

[54] Dopamine is one of the chemicals which helps us to 'retain' information.
[55] Krashen, S.D. (1982) *Principles and Practice in Second Language Acquisition.* Oxford: Pergamon.
[56] Nevid, J.S. (2013) *Psychology: Concepts and Applications* (4th edition). New York: St Johns University, p. 61

Jeanne Ellis Ormrod, in her book[57] *Essentials of Educational Psychology*, highlights:

'The following general principles which describe how motivation interrelate behaviour, cognition, and learning.

Motivation directs behaviour toward particular goals [...]

Motivation increases effort and persistence and activities [...]

Motivation affects cognitive processes [...]

Motivation determines what consequences are reinforcing and punishing [...]

Motivation often leads to improved performance [...]

Intrinsic motivation is more beneficial than extrinsic motivation [...]'

As Neurolanguage coaches, we know that motivation is a necessary ingredient for any learning process. If we think back to where coaching really originates, namely the sports coach, we have a very clear image of the 'coach', who is constantly motivating, animating and inspiring the sportsman or sportswoman to achieve their goal. This goal may be the cup, winning the race or even just winning the game, but the motivation to win or to achieve is there. This is what the Neurolanguage coach imitates, and principally what we strive to find is that intrinsic, inner-self motivating factor or factors that are going to keep our language learner wanting to learn more and more and more. Obviously, the more progress and success the learner feels and witnesses, the more that motivation is going to be fuelled. So, there needs to be an extremely skillful coaching conversation touching upon what the key motivation is for our learner to learn (see section on motivation in Part IV).

Personally, I have witnessed my own learning motivation with all the languages I speak, each time a different feeling driving that motivation.

---

[57] Ormrod, J.E. (2008) *Essentials of Educational Psychology: Big Ideas to Guide Effective Teaching* (2nd edition). Boston: Pearson, pp. 384–386.

Learning French at school was something I enjoyed. However, my motivation drastically increased when I developed a very close friendship with a French lady, and that propelled me into realms of the language that school had never provided. I remember thinking at about the age of 15, 'Wow, I am having girly conversations in French!'

My motivation to learn Spanish was because I fell in love with a certain gentleman and I definitely have to admit that was a key driving motivator for me to become fluent (also knowing that he would not learn English!).

My motivation to learn Italian developed through working and living in Italy, again quite strong motivation. I have to confess that my motivation to learn German was in fact extremely low in the beginning, due to the fact that I put Italian first, plus I found it difficult to connect to the German language. Some years later, when my Italian was flowing, I started to come into German much more and, indeed, my motivation increased. So, I personally have experienced what 'extreme' or 'not enough' motivation did for me on my language learning journey.

This means that initially, when the language coaching engagement begins, the coach and the learner should have a very deep conversation regarding the learner's intrinsic motivation. The coach has to be skilled enough in this conversation to find that intrinsic motivation: something that really energises the learner to learn. It might not be enough just to hear the learner say that they are motivated to learn English for work. A more powerful question behind this would be 'How would speaking fluent English at work change your life?', and the coachee may respond that it could bring a promotion, a relocation or even more frequent travel. Once this intrinsic motivation has been ascertained, the coach should constantly bring the coachee back to the vision of such motivation and keep reminding the learner of, and connecting with, his/her motivation throughout the learning process.

Another essential aspect which will assist in maintaining motivation will be the continual setting of language goals and subsequent and periodic review of these. Goal-setting and review will help the learner to register and recognise progress and success and thus keep the coachee focused on his/her ultimate vision and motivation to learn or improve the language.

> So, yes, motivation is crucial for optimal learning.

(Later I will go into more detail on how to conduct those coaching conversations on motivation.)

3. Energy flows where attention goes

A well-known expression, seemingly originating from Hawaiian tradition, is the expression 'energy flows where attention goes'. It is the perfect way of describing how the brain strengthens and reinforces neural networks. The more attention we give to the task at hand, the stronger the neural connections relating to that task. Conversely, the expression 'use it or lose it' also reflects how our brain connections weaken when we do not practise something enough. The Neurolanguage coach is always fully aware that we need enough attention and focus from the learner at all times to ensure the firing and wiring in the hippocampus.

This not only means that our learner should be free of any distractions, for example mobile phones, emails or telephone calls, but also the learner should be engaged and attentive enough with active, fun, interesting, inspiring learning activities. Variety and novelty can keep the attention level high, as well as visualisation, interactive discussion, relevant and real topics: topics that connect to and affect the learner personally will also ensure attention levels. Additionally, the coach should be aware if the learner seems to have other things on his/her mind that could potentially interfere with the learning process. At the start of the session the coach could address these issues by saying that he/she can see that the coachee has a lot on their mind and point out that the session together will only last for 60 minutes (or whatever the programmed time is for the session) and then ask the coachee how he/she would feel if they could leave those issues aside just for this programmed time, so that full attention can be dedicated to the learning process in order to achieve the maximum optimal learning from that session.

I also believe that as coaches, with our heightened levels of empathy, we become sensitive to when we 'lose' our learner. Some years ago, I had a client whose focus and attention, now and then, (I could literally see and sense) drifted into issues that were on his mind. I say that I could see this, because it was almost like his eyes would glaze over; even when he was responding to me he had the glazed look, and the response would get slower. As soon as I noticed this, I would check in with him and just say, 'I am sensing that your mind is drifting to other issues and I would just like to check with you if you would like us to have a quick break and if you would like to get up and explore something. Just to give your brain a little rest so that we can come back after this small pause with full attention into the language again.' Sometimes he would take up the offer and other times he would then pull himself back without me saying anything, pushing those thoughts away and becoming fully present into the language again.

I had another client who one day left me totally speechless. I had been with this client for some years already, but that particular day, in the middle of our session, he took me by surprise by telling me that he was a 'power-napper' and he desperately needed to take a power-nap! The next minute he had fallen asleep, right there in front of me in his chair! Well, at first I could not believe it, then I realised that he really was asleep and I started to look around the room, thinking, 'Okay, should I just sit here? Should I leave? How long will he be out'? So, I just got on with some agenda setting and checking my next schedules, and about ten minutes later, he 'came to'. Believe it or not, we then picked up and continued from where we had left off, as if nothing had happened, and he was completely lucid and giving the language his full attention again.

So, as a coach, accept whatever it takes to retain and ensure your learner's attention. We know attention is crucial and the neural networks that get the most attention will be reinforced.

4. Performing brain should take over

If you have gone through the process of learning a language, you will know that there are various steps from being a beginner in that language to achieving fluency and mastery. If we compare mastery of the language with driving a car, we can see that the two are in fact comparable. After many years of driving a car, an experienced driver performs the activity from a subconscious program, and no conscious thought is given to any of the necessary tasks for driving that car. Achieving absolute fluency in a foreign language is exactly the same: the fluent speaker gives no thought to the language spoken; it simply flows from the subconscious with no need for translation or even thought to the language being spoken.

As learners of languages, we do go through the uncomfortable stages of firstly needing to really concentrate and think about grammar constructions, sentence structure and how all of this fits together. Then we go to the awareness stage, where we are frequently translating the native language into the target language in our minds. At some point, parts of the language start to become automatically programmed in such a way that we do not need to even think about these parts any more; the language just spontaneously comes out. Often, the more we can discuss topics we are passionate about, or topics that are extremely real and personal to us in the target language, the more we start to forget that we are speaking a new language and the more we go into the performing brain and further away from the thinking brain. As Neurolanguage coaches, we are more conscious of the performing brain phenomenon and so will try to steer our coachee into that status as much as we can. There have been times when I myself have been with clients who have continuously flowed with 'their' topic for 60 minutes in English. At the end of the session I have asked them if they realised they had been speaking solidly for 60 minutes in English and most of them replied that they honestly had not! This, for me, was pure confirmation that the client had been in his/her performing brain during that hour.[58]

---

[58] *The Inner Game of Tennis* by Timothy Gallwey (1997, Random House) discusses the phenomena of performing brain vs. thinking brain.

One of the real questions for the coach is how to get our learner into, firstly, a relaxed state of mind, so that the limbic system is calm and happy, and secondly, interested enough to be flowing with the topic and allowing the language to come out. Obviously, you're going to say to me that, of course, if there are words missing and grammar parts missing, the learner will struggle, but even in these cases, if the learner feels safe enough to try synonyms or alternative expressions to express themselves and the coach allows this without finishing off sentences, interrupting or trying to interfere in any way with the conversation, then the learner builds the trust to go with the flow. The whole philosophy behind language coaching is to be predominantly engaged in interactive, brain-friendly conversations. I would even suggest that the ratio of talking time should be 70% coachee and 30% coach. The coach is the sounding board, the motivator, the facilitator, the stimulator or 'provocateur' of language.

If you have ever been to a Zumba class, you will witness how the instructors never ever teach the steps. The beginner walks into the room and just has to 'do it'. I am fascinated every time a new person joins the Zumba class, because I observe each time just how quickly people 'do it'. It is absolutely amazing. Somehow I firmly believe from my own experience, and from witnessing others, that learning by doing is one of the most powerful ways of learning. Being thrown in at the deep end (may I add, though, with an extremely calm and peaceful limbic system and not in any way under threat situations) produces great results – but as I said, the coach must ensure there is no stress or threat in the situation.

> So, I do believe that getting our learner into the 'just do it' brain would mean that the subconscious programs of the language take over and stimulate the language to start to flow naturally.

5. Chunk it down

We already mentioned that learning a language can potentially throw a learner into a threat state and a negative limbic reaction. We already talked about the fact that language learning is never-ending, and so the

Neurolanguage coach will be constantly explaining to the learner that the language will be broken down into pieces to be built back up again in a block-building process. The language coaching engagement will consist of a rolling process of setting goals, working towards them and then achieving them to then set further goals, work towards them and achieve them, and so on.

As a language expert, the Neurolanguage coach will also be delivering any grammatical topic relating to that target language in and through a coaching conversation. This coaching conversation will actually reflect a step-by-step, chunk it down, build it back up process of the grammatical topic. It is essential for the coach to expertly know how to break down a given grammar topic, so that during that key conversation relating to that grammar area, the coach and coachee will always be at the same place and at the same time. In fact, non-grammatical topics should also follow the same principle of 'chunk it down'. Whatever the task, whatever the project, whatever the topic, always break it down so that the brain remains calm and retains the feeling of being capable of achieving what needs to be achieved.

> So, chunking it down is an essential principle for a Neurolanguage coach to follow.

6. Constant connection to target language

We know that the brain learns through association, so, following this law of association, the brain is constantly endeavouring to connect new information to existing information or existing networks within the brain. It is almost as if the brain is looking for where to connect new information into the existing filing cabinets within our minds.

My own language learning experience has helped me to understand the importance associating languages has, and wherever possible I absolutely encourage and promote this. Having learnt Latin, Greek and French at school, all three languages helped me to come into Spanish at the age of 15 when I taught myself the language with my father's 'teach yourself Spanish' books. Of course, as I mentioned before, I had the best motivation anyone can have for learning a language – I was in love with a Spaniard. My first letters to him were indeed an interesting language mix. There was a definite hotchpotch of Latin and French mixed with my attempts at Spanish, which then over a period of two years metamorphosed into excellent written Spanish. My consistent connecting and associating of words and grammar from Latin and French really helped me to come quickly into the Spanish language – and I never had one Spanish lesson in my life!

Years later, I was to experience the same learning by association and disassociation (false friends!) when I transformed my Spanish knowledge into Italian. I never had one Italian lesson! I just actively began to learn by myself, assisted by frequent periods of time in Italy and then associating my Latin language pool knowledge, connecting back to my French, Spanish and Latin. It did, in fact, only take me approximately six months to become fairly fluent in Italian. A peculiarity worth highlighting here is that at some point, after having lived in Spain for 12 years with such a high degree of integration into Spanish life and the Spanish language, Spanish has, in fact, become almost like my base language when learning or speaking other languages. Even more fascinating is the fact that when I speak Italian or French, people often mistakenly think that I am Spanish, because I have a heavy Spanish accent when speaking other Latin-based languages. Just to add a funny story, about seven years ago I was driving at Lake Garda, Italy, and I was stopped by the Italian police. I presented the officer with my English passport, my German driving licence and spoke with him in Italian. With an extremely puzzled expression he proceeded to ask me, 'Are you English?' 'Yes', I replied. 'Then, why do you speak Italian with a Spanish accent?'

My own explanation of this is that somehow my brain has developed a Latin languages pool with a predominance in Spanish. This has enabled me to connect not only with French and Italian but also Catalan and some Portuguese, as well as understanding and recognising Latin elements that sometimes appear in other languages, for example Romanian.

Having an extremely strong Latin pool, however, somehow hindered me coming into the German language. When I was converting my Italian, I was in fact living in Germany and for years was trying to improve my German, but it proved to be extremely difficult for my brain. One day I reflected upon what the difficulty could be, as with all my other languages I had had a relatively easy transition, and I realised that I needed to shift away from my Latin pool and I needed to connect back to my mother tongue, English, to associate the Germanic roots in English with modern German. Once I understood this, the connections started to flow.

One example of this is when only one or two of the letters change, giving the clue to the same word or a similar word. For example, if we take the German D, this is often replaced in English by the TH or the German T with the English D.[59] For example:

thunder – donner

thumb – daumen

thirst – durst

dream – träume

drop – tropfen

reindeer – rentier

Sometimes just a simple insight of a letter change can lead the brain instantly into associating vocabulary across languages.

A Neurolanguage coach should be constantly assisting the coachee to make these connections. Let me give you another example: just this summer, I was refreshing my French with one of my certified language coaches, and she gave me the most amazing insight that I had not seen before. She explained that the circumflex accent in French often reflected a missing S from the word, which once existed in old French,[60]

---

[59] This change is known as the High German consonant shift.

[60] Corresponding Norman French words, which in English then retained the lost consonant.

and often the word in English is the same word, but with an S. For example:

hôpital – hospital

forêt – forest

côte – coast

bête – beast

dépôt – depot, originating from the Latin word 'deposit'!

What an amazing insight! I had never realised that before, and suddenly my whole French vocabulary has opened up to give me a direct link from potential words that I don't know or didn't think that I knew, that just by adding that S may lead me directly to the English translation.

Moving on now to another incredible instant booster for beginners learning a Latin-based language: did you know that just by asking a learner to think about all the English words that end in –ION, you may have just given that learner the key to hundreds of words instantly in Spanish, French and Italian? And also in other languages?! For example: education, religion, profession, illusion and demonstration are all easily converted into those same words, maybe with a slightly different spelling and pronunciation, but essentially the SAME words!

So, with this language approach we have to constantly provoke the thought process of connecting and associating in our learner wherever possible. In some ways, this is one of the foundations of the Michel Thomas Method, where target language is linked to equivalents in the native language, and Thomas highlights Latin influences in English to allow learners to incorporate existing vocabulary into the target language. However, Thomas said that this use is an 'effective gimmick to get started, but it is not the method'.[61]

---

[61] Woodsmall, M., and Woodsmall, W. (2008) *The Future of Learning: The Michel Thomas Method: Freeing Minds One at a Time.* Great Falls, VA: Next Step Press, p. 148.

On the other hand, connecting target to native could also lead to false connections, as we know with the phenomena of false friends in a language. For example, the word 'embarrassed' in English could lead to an association with 'embarazada' in Spanish, which actually means pregnant – a very embarrassing mix-up to make! Therefore, the coach has to also bring to the attention of the learner the connections that lead to missed connections. I have to say that in all the languages that I personally know, the most remarkable false friend for English learners is almost the same word in so many languages, yet not English! This is the word 'simpatico' in Spanish, in French 'sympathique', in German 'sympathisch' and in Italian 'simpatico'. The word itself remains very similar across these languages, but simply does not 'work' in English. The closest English translation is 'nice' or 'pleasant', when referring to how nice a person is and with no bearing on the Latin-rooted meaning whatsoever! Most Spanish, French, German and Italian learners of English get it wrong, as their brain automatically associates with 'sympathic', or 'sympathetic' – which obviously in English has a totally different meaning. It is amazing to witness how the brain primarily tries to go to what it knows and what is the most familiar expression first.

Having a language coach who fully understands where these connections work and where they don't work speeds up the learning process. Learners have instant insight or 'Aha!' moments, which more often than not they **never ever** forget. It is almost like the brain instantly 'gets' it!

In this way, the language coach will be constantly provoking connections, constantly asking the right questions, leading the brain to that associative process, really helping the brain to connect. This is also the same for grammar points: how is the grammar the same, how is it different, how would the coachee explain the similarity or difference, etc.

As previously mentioned, I have experienced this through my own learning and I have witnessed over the last ten years how quickly my learners connect. In addition, I have received feedback from all the language coaches that have certified with me and practise this approach, and they all state that they are also witnessing the impressive speed with which learners grasp the connections. Yes, this does go against the grain of the more traditional ways of teaching languages where the philosophy is that the mother tongue should not be used, and on the one hand, I totally agree that as much target language as possible should be used. However, where necessary, where possible and where applicable, it is essential to bring in native/target insight.

You know, this approach can even be used with regard to mistakes. Most of our target language mistakes actually come from mother tongue interference, or, as I sometimes call it, a 'mother tongue infection'. This means that the brain goes directly and automatically to what it already knows and, more often than not, the brain will pull out a word from the native language when it does not know the word in the target language. An excellent example of this is in German, specifically the word 'als', which means 'than'. When making comparisons, many Germans would say 'John is taller as Peter.' Notice their brain has directly gone to 'as' due to the similarity with the word 'als'. Usually when I ask a learner about this mistake and point out the similarity they instantly understand the reason for choosing the word 'as' and they start to develop an in-built alarm regarding that misconnection to then move into the correct use with the word 'than'. This is only one example of thousands. The language coach should deftly steer the conversation, asking their learner where a mistake is from and seeking the origin, or potential origin, of that mistake.

In conclusion, in my humble opinion, constantly connecting our learner with both target and native language is essential for the language learning process. I welcome the research led by Kirsten Weber at the University of Nijmegen is conducting regarding the connection of native to target language[62] and welcome further scientific evidence to prove this further. By the way, it is always worthwhile asking a learner what other languages they already know, because they may

---

[62] Weber, K., Christiansen, M.K., Magnus Petersson, K.M., Indefrey, P., and Hagoort, P. (2016) *fMRI syntactic and lexical repetition effects reveal the initial stages of learning a new language.* Journal of Neuroscience 36, 6872–6880.

even be able to connect other language knowledge with the new target language. Again, referring to my own language experience, I was intrigued to discover that in fact there are quite a few Greek origin words in Russian and certain similarities between the Greek and the Cyrillic alphabets. This has greatly assisted me to instantly recognise some words in my quest to learn some Russian.

> So, constant provocation to connect target to native can greatly enhance the language learning process.

7. Know thy brain and understand that the brain loves habit!

Personally, the more I know about my own brain, the more I understand myself. As I look back through my life, I can understand certain reactions, certain situations and certain behaviours that I can now explain and fully comprehend. Perhaps one of the most interesting insights for me is that my brain definitely needs the real and practical to be able to absorb and understand the learning. I can see that I was an excellent learner of theory, but then had great difficulty transforming that theory into practice, and I really needed an extreme personal reason or motivation for my brain to want to come into that practical understanding.

There have been numerous other insights that I have had (as previously stated) regarding my language learning experience, as well as recognising deep subconscious brain patterns that I had unwittingly assumed as a child, which then had an impact on most of my life until now, when I have been able to recognise these patterns and alter them.

Additionally, through the years, I have recognised how I react to fear; how my limbic system used to throw me into panic every time I got on an aeroplane, and how I then discovered how to calm my fear of flying to finally reach the breakthrough of now flying with absolutely no fear whatsoever. I forced myself to fly every week by taking work in Italy and working in Germany, and then I trained my brain to go into a calm, meditative state every time I got on a plane. After a few times, it started to become automatic. Now, I thoroughly enjoy flying and I am also capable of getting on a plane and being so relaxed and so peaceful that I fall asleep. That has to be one of my greatest achievements in life: the battle of overcoming an extreme fear.

The reason I am saying all this is because I have realised that the more I know about my brain, the more effectively I can get my mind to function, whether in my thought processes, learning processes or whatever I am putting my mind to at any given time. I have also noticed over the years that the more I share about the knowledge of the brain with my clients, the more fascinated and engaged they become, and in addition they start to understand more about how *they* themselves operate and how *they* learn. We have to remember that everybody's brain is different. Every brain is one of a kind! The learner sitting in front of us each time will be absolutely unique and will probably learn in a totally different way to the next learner in front of us. In this way, the Neurolanguage coach shares, whenever relevant, information regarding:

- how the brain makes connections
- how the limbic system may react
- how the brain can block during the learning process
- how to keep attention high
- how to keep motivation high
- and any relevant information that could really assist the learner to know and understand him/herself better.

Above all, we need to remember that the brain is, in essence, a creature of habit. In 2003 I made a life decision to move to Germany, to a country which was totally new to me. I could not speak the language and had no idea whatsoever of how my new life would be. One of the greatest, and at the same time simplest, of tips was given to me from an amazing source (one could say of Divine Intervention!): 'Create habits and routines as quickly as possible and your transition into your new life will be smooth.' I consciously followed that advice and by day three had started to instil my new routines and, sure enough, within one week I was feeling settled and my brain was calm.

So, knowing about our own brain and respecting its nature as a 'creature of habit and subconscious programmer' will greatly assist our learner to get to know his/her brain.

In summary, these are the seven underlying principles of neuroscience which are constants within the Neurolanguage Coaching process:

➢ A constantly calm brain state is absolutely essential.

➢ Motivation is crucial for optimal learning.

➢ Ensure the learner's attention. We know that it is crucial, because the neural networks that get the most attention will become stronger.

➢ Get the learner into the 'just do it' brain. This means that the subconscious programs of the language take over and stimulate the language to start to flow naturally.

➢ Chunk it down! Whether this refers to the process of language learning or the mechanical grammatical breakdown of the language itself.

➢ Constant provocation to connect target language to native can greatly enhance the language learning process.

➢ Knowing about our own brain and respecting its nature as a 'creature of habit and subconscious programmer' will greatly assist our learner to get to know his/her brain.

Part III

What is coaching?

Seemingly, the first use of the term 'coaching' can be traced back to 1840–50 and used in the sense of a tutor, considered to be someone who carries a student through an exam.[63]

Subsequently, the term 'coach' has been and is profoundly used in relation to sports and the figure of the 'sports coach' is that inspiring, motivating, strong, determined personality, pushing us to achieve the cup, sprint the fastest, jump the highest. Ironically, a sports coach today would need to take further steps to become a sports teacher with recognised teaching qualifications, whereas in the language world we are actually doing the opposite – that is, teachers are enhancing the teaching process by becoming qualified coaches.

In the 1990s, coaching began to develop into an independent discipline, and professional associations were set up to develop recognised training standards within the coaching profession. One of these recognised associations is the International Coach Federation, founded in 1995, which defines coaching as 'partnering with clients in a thought-provoking and creative process that inspires them to maximise their personal and professional potential'.

There are various definitions of coaching these days. Here are some examples:

- 'Coaching is the art of facilitating the performance, learning and development of another.'[64]

---

[63] Definition according to *Online Etymology Dictionary:* http://www.etymonline.com /index.php?term=coach.

[64] Downey, M. (2003) *Effective Coaching: Lessons from the Coach's Coach.* Knutsford: Texere.

- 'Unlocking a person's potential to maximise their own performance. It is helping them to learn rather than teaching them.'[65]
- 'A collaborative, solution focused, result-orientated and systematic process in which the coach facilitates the enhancement of work performance, life experience, self-directed learning and personal growth of the coachee.'[66]
- 'A professional partnership between a qualified coach and an individual or team that supports the achievement of extra-ordinary results, based on goals set by the individual or team.'[67]

Nowadays, it really can be said that the coaching profession and industry is continually growing and spreading into a vast array of disciplines. Coaching is extensively used in the corporate world where leadership coaching, executive coaching, business coaching and team coaching are commonly pursued. Additionally, over recent years we hear a lot of new types of coaching, for example, health coaching, spiritual coaching, career coaching, systemic coaching, relationship coaching, interview coaching – the list is endless, and coaching appears to be invading all walks of life.

In a nutshell, coaching could be described as an ongoing conversation between the coach and the coachee (face-to-face or by telephone/online) which assists the coachee to explore (an) aspect(s) of the coachee's life to enhance, improve, assist the coachee to achieve short or long-term goals which the coachee then sets as realistic targets. In essence, coaching is a practical tool for personal exploration and development; the coach facilitates conversation through active listening, powerful questions, coaching presence and awareness,

---

[65] Whitmore, J. (2002) *Coaching for Performance: Growing People, Performance and Purpose.* London: Nicholas Brealey.

[66] Grant, A.M. (1999) *Enhancing Performance through Coaching: The Promise of CBT.* Paper presented at the First State Conference of the Australian Association of Cognitive Behavioural Therapy (NSW), Sydney.

[67] ICF 2005

displaying empathy and generating trust. This enables the coachee to enhance or improve aspects of his/her life or reach solutions and come to his/her own conclusions about life dilemmas and decisions.

These are some of the principles of being a great coach:

- Excellent active listener
- Empathetic at all times
- Expert at posing the right questions at the right moment
- Capable of creating mood, climate and safe setting for coachee
- Sees the coachee as equal
- Engages the coachee to be motivated
- Is a flexible resource for the coachee
- Allows the coachee to feel in control of his/her process
- Provokes ongoing thoughts
- Responds with emotion and empathy
- Able to deliver continuous positive feedback and acknowledgement
- Holds absolutely no judgements
- Sustains great use of coaching conversations
- Recognises his/her own limitations
- Is honest at all times.

At this point, I would also like to clarify what coaching is not. Coaching is not therapy, counselling or psychotherapy of any kind, nor is it consulting or training or mentoring. Therapy and counselling are normally about analysing the past and will often focus on an event or aspect of a person's past and work on potentially, for example, comprehending, healing, resolving, improving or recovering.

Therapy or counselling can be said to be a form of guidance, giving advice or providing a course of action. A counsellor's training background may be a variety of fields, including (and in no way limited to) education, health care and psychology.

In contrast, coaching deals with the whole person's performance/ aspects of life and is primarily present-oriented. Fundamentally, coaching deals with the 'now' and the immediate future, although a coach should 'fact-find' to ascertain the current situation to gain an insight into how past events may have influenced and shaped a person's life or current situation. In other words, coaching should not reflect on the coachee's past to work out and solve psychological problems or issues, and nor is it instruction, training or mentoring, nor does it transfer new vocational skills or knowledge.

I would like to add that there are possibly different perceptions regarding the coaching profession across the world. The 'coaching' I have described above is what I would call the American/British perception of this profession, which I believe is now the worldwide predominant view. Eight years ago, when I started to talk about language coaching in Germany, the Germans had a completely different perception and considered 'coaching' a 'hush-hush' process, not to be spoken of, as it seemingly implied that someone had a 'problem'. I was amazed at this perception!

Language coaching and Neurolanguage Coaching

Over the last decade language coaching has evolved, and today more and more language teachers and trainers call themselves language coaches without any formal coaching qualification or certification.

So, what are the differences between coaching, language coaching and Neurolanguage Coaching?

Well, we have just taken a look at coaching, which really centres and focuses upon personal questions, issues, dilemmas and/or goals. Language coaching, however, must necessarily have as its main focus – a target language that is being learnt, improved or developed – and there must be a definite focus on 'language'. So, in theory, what is language coaching? Well, it could be said that language coaching transports elements and principles from the coaching world and integrates them into the language learning process. Such elements and principles may be coaching models or the structure of a coaching engagement, which would involve goal-setting processes and action-setting processes together with a setting of time periods and a clear management of coaching engagements. The coach, ideally, would possess coaching training and would embrace the principles and ethics from coaching standards, such as those set by the International Coach Federation, and would also display the full array of coach competencies that a qualified coach would possess.

I do sometimes hear confusion between coaching and language coaching, and for this reason I do think it is essential to be clear on the definitions of both. The confusion is fuelled by language trainers conducting 'life-coaching' sessions in a target language and calling this language coaching. I beg to differ. This is life-coaching in a target language. The critical point is where IS the focus of the session? Is it solving/resolving a dilemma/setting a personal goal or improving the target language? In such a case, I would suggest there has to be a clear delineation of the purpose and focus of the session, so that both the coach and the coachee are fully clear of the focus and desired outcomes of the session, and in this way the expectations of the client may be met. In addition, I might add that there is probably a difference in pricing, depending on whether a life-coaching session or a language coaching session is being conducted.

Now, we have to ask the question 'What is the concept of Neurolanguage Coaching and what is it trying to achieve?' In my opinion, it takes language coaching one step further as it incorporates all the elements and principles from the coaching world which I mentioned above. Additionally, it adopts a coaching conversation that is absolutely brain-friendly and, in addition, brings in principles from the latest findings of neuroscience and in turn enlightens the learner as to how the brain operates, functions and learns.

In 2012, I created the definition[68] of Neurolanguage Coaching as:

> Neurolanguage Coaching is the efficient and fast transfer of language knowledge with sustainable effects from the Language Coach to the Language Coachee facilitated by brain-based coaching and coaching principles as vehicles.

In this respect, Neurolanguage Coaching is the continuous flow of language training constantly interacting with aspects of brain-based coaching and aspects of traditional coaching. These all enhance the transfer of language knowledge with the constant awareness of how the brain makes connections and creates long-term memories during the learning process, consolidating the new target language.

In summary, it can be said that:

- Neurolanguage Coaching is always orientated to attention, focus, long-term memory and consolidation of language learning.

---

[68] Paling, R.M. (2012) *What is Language Coaching?* at
http://www.languagecoachingcertification.com/language-coaching/

- Neurolanguage Coaching is an extensive dialogue or coaching conversation around language to facilitate language learning.
- Neurolanguage Coaching blends language transfer with brain-friendly coaching and traditional coaching principles as set out by the International Coaching Federation.
- Neurolanguage Coaching is not teaching, but will inherently include grammatical and theoretical parts of language teaching and some teaching elements.

What Neurolanguage Coaching is not!

At this point it could be interesting (and necessary) to clarify what Neurolanguage Coaching is not. It is not:

1. Just working through a language book.

In general, Neurolanguage Coaching is really about the coach being the resource. The whole engagement should consist of continuous coaching conversations in which there is an interplay between the mechanical side of the language (grammar) and the mastery side of the language (application). Of course, materials can be introduced; however, these should only be used as provocations to trigger the coaching conversations and not used as the main and only focus of a session.

2. A traditional teacher/student relationship.

There is definitely a movement away from the traditional teacher–student relationship. In the past, however, there has been a certain 'superiority' of the teacher, with a more passive role of the learner. This is drastically changed in the coach–coachee relationship, which is a relationship of equal status. In a session there should ideally be at least 70% spoken participation from the learner in relation to a 30% input from the coach. This ensures that the learner is incredibly active throughout a Neurolanguage Coaching engagement. I have had countless clients who have complained to me about previous trainers who spent most of their session talking about themselves and 'hogging' the conversation. This totally defeats the object of language learning and can also potentially hinder the learner even more from speaking.

3. A life-coaching session.

We already mentioned that Neurolanguage Coaching is NOT a life-coaching session. There is a necessary focus and connection to language learning, whether this is a mechanical focus on the grammatical side of the language or a mastery focus regarding the application of the target language. The application may be, for instance, how to deliver presentations in English (as the target language), as this still retains a language focus. It could, however, go beyond this and also include questions regarding delivery, style or overcoming nerves. Yet the focal point would still be enhancing the final presentation in the target language.

In my own experience, I have indeed had clients who come to the language coaching session and want to discuss their personal problems. I know this happens daily to thousands of language trainers, teachers, instructors or coaches, and many of the people who have taken my course share this experience. In this particular case, it is necessary for the language coach to bring the focus and attention of the coachee back into the language learning. This can be done quite subtly by firstly asking the coachee whether he/she would like to continue with the same personal conversation, but that 'you', the coach, would like to analyse the language. This means that you would take note of any mistakes and then every now and then, break from the conversation to talk about the language that had been used and the mistakes that were observed. In this way, the coach gently but firmly brings the focal point back into the mission of language learning. Conversely, the coach may highlight to the coachee that the session is about improving the language and gently persuade the coachee to come back into a language focus by introducing the goals that have been previously agreed by the coachee.

4. A psychological process like therapy or mentoring.

As mentioned above, Neurolanguage Coaching has nothing to do with therapy or mentoring. Interestingly, when I first started to develop the concept of language coaching and Neurolanguage Coaching in

Germany in the mid-2000s, new concepts were frowned upon by certain HR employees and purchasing department employees. It was considered absolutely taboo to put coaching together with language because in Germany coaching was considered to be an extremely confidential process which no one should talk about. In addition, only professional coaches who had studied a higher university degree or diploma were 'accepted'. In this respect, when I began to introduce coaching together with language, following the American and UK concept of coaching, some Germans did not like it, nor did they accept it. I later understood that this was also the same phenomena in other countries, for example France. In one meeting (which actually lasted two hours) with a purchase manager in Germany in 2011, I was attacked, insulted, humiliated and shot down for connecting coaching to language. My secretary at that time was with me in the meeting and afterwards we both sat in my car, looked at each other and burst into tears! Believe me, the way in which that man spoke to me will never be forgotten! Nevertheless, this meeting was key: it brought out my sheer determination and desire to prove that language coaching existed and it served as the motivational driver for me to clearly crystallise, delineate and define this new concept of language coaching and then to further enhance it with the principles of neuroscience and Neurolanguage Coaching.

5. A consultancy session.

There are many extremely qualified professionals who are now turning to the field of language coaching and Neurolanguage Coaching. Some are lawyers and specialise in the field of legal language coaching. Others are ex-professionals from the finance industry, accountants, investment bankers, etc. and all of these ex-professionals are bringing their professional expertise into a specialised language coaching arena. These particular individuals will always have to ensure that language coaching engagements remain as such, and that they do not wander into any type of consultancy at any time. Consultancy would probably require professional indemnity insurance and, in addition, consultancy would command significantly higher fees.

6. Just a chat!

Neurolanguage Coaching is not about just having a conversational chat with clients. It definitely may be the case that our learners do want to focus on the spoken aspects of language much more than the written, listening or comprehension parts of language. However, at all times, the coach must ensure that any conversation has a definite focus as well as a definite structure. In addition, the conversation must have intervals where the interaction comes into analysing the language that has been used, the difficulties faced, the positive sides of the language used and any other observations that can help the learner to comprehend and correct or enhance the vocabulary and the grammar used.

The bottom line is that all conversation must have an underlying purpose and direction that is clearly voiced and steered by the coachee. This keeps the brain focused on a clear purpose and desired outcome for that conversation.

The differences between language teaching and Neurolanguage Coaching

In reality, Neurolanguage Coaching aims to be much, much more than language teaching or training. However, it must never be forgotten that there is a theoretical and grammatical part of language learning in which the Neurolanguage coach will have to explain grammatical principles and constructions, and the coach will often need to touch upon a necessary teaching or training element of language learning.

The difference in Neurolanguage Coaching comes from:

- how the material is delivered
- how the Neurolanguage coach captures the attention of the coachee
- how the Neurolanguage coach facilitates brain connections through associations and encourages long-term retention of the material
- how the Neurolanguage coach builds rapport and dialogues with the coachee so that the brain is never triggered into a threat status response.

In 2013 I wrote an article to distinguish the differences between language coaching and language teaching.[69] These differences were echoed in an article by Dimitris Zeppos in a table (see opposite) demonstrating the principle differences between language teaching and language coaching.[70] In fact, in the left-hand column we can

---

[68] Paling, R.M. (2014) *The differences between language teaching and language coaching.* Research Chronicler 2(6), 13–19.
http://research-chronicler.com/reschro/pdf/v2i6/2602.pdf.

[70] Zeppos, D. (2014) *Profiling neurolanguage coaches worldwide – a case study.* World Journal of Education 4(6), 26–41.

clearly see the elements belonging to Neurolanguage Coaching in contrast to the elements of traditional style teaching fascinatingly, over these last three years I am in contact with language teachers worldwide, and there does seem to be a progressive phenomenon of experienced and mature teachers who are naturally and intuitively introducing elements from language coaching without realising what they are doing. Upon completing my course to become a Neurolanguage coach, these intuitive teachers have then been able to realise what exactly they had been doing and also to realise the full impact and implications this had on the brain of the learner.

In essence, teachers that gain knowledge of traditional coaching and brain-friendly coaching conversations and then transform into Neurolanguage coaches become:

- aware of how the brain learns
- aware of their own impact as an educator on the learner s brain
- sensitive to 'limbic threat reactions' of the brain
- provocative – provoking brain connections
- experts at powerful brain-friendly conversations
- experts at active listening, in particular active listening on various different levels, bearing in mind that the Neurolanguage coach is listening to content as well as linguistic abilities, mistakes, grammar and sentence constructions
- much more empathetic
- aware of coaching ethics and principles
- masters in goal-setting conversations and no longer tell their coachees what to do
- absolutely non-directive, less demonstrative and much more interactive and passive (as the learner takes the role as the active participant)
- the catalyst, facilitator and sounding board
- structured and orientated towards focus and attention, always artfully steering the brain into a focused 'reason' for all conversations.

69

Table 1 Comparison between Characteristics of Neurolanguage Coaching and Traditional Language Teaching

Language coaching	Language teaching
• Active learning • Motivation takes top priority • Empathy	• Passive
• Coach has ability to keep client engaged, motivated, valued and committed	• It could sometimes be described as a mainly one-way process
• Client takes responsibility and ownership • Flexible and self-directed	• Book related – following chapters and the order of language learning books
• Normally no books are used	• Often limited to materials/books used
• There is an equal status of coach and learner • There is an awareness of limitations • Matches the needs of the client	• Teacher takes the role of the expert, denoting a superior status • The relationship between teacher and the learner is often not so close, nor is it a realistic or personalised experience • Often encompasses a more formal approach
• 'Teaching' is kept to a minimum • Continuous feedback and acknowledgement • Stimulates reflexion	• Instructive and mandatory • Directional • Demonstrative
• Coach has the ability to adapt to the client • Client focused and tailor-made	• With groups – often trial and error – not tailored to individuals • Often the subject must be learnt, so the teacher is interested in the topic but the learner is not

Language coaching	Language teaching
• One objective is to maximise the potential of the learner	• Often does not take into account the social context and cultural interaction of the learner
• Focus on cost-effectiveness	• Normally not cost-effective and no awareness relating to cost-effectiveness

Part IV

The process and structure of Neurolanguage Coaching

The theoretical spiral learning process

The process of a Neurolanguage Coaching engagement moves forward in cycles. This is reflected in the PROGRESS©[71] model, which I created in 2012 and which clearly explains the progressive cyclical learning process. The model can be used to reflect the process to the learner so that they can fully appreciate this.

PROGRESS stands for:

P – Practise

R – Repeat

O – Ongoing

G – Goals

R – Remember

E – Emotions

S – Success

S – Start again

Broadly speaking, the process involves initiating from a two-tier goal-setting process. The goals are set by the coachee, who also indicates a realistic time period in which to achieve those goals. As such, the learning process commences. The goals are worked on during the given time period and once this period comes to an end a goal review is held to check on the coachee's progress. If the coachee feels that the goals have

---

[71] ©Rachel Marie Paling 2012.

been reached, then new goals are set and the whole process recommences. The cyclical process from goal-setting to goal-setting, involves chunking down the language into bite-size goals, which, as we know, keeps the limbic system calm and the brain able to focus better.

The coachee **Practises** and **Repeats** the **Ongoing Goals** that are continually being set. Through this practice and repetition, the coachee **Remembers**, and positive **Emotions** ensure the right chemical processes in the brain to assist the long-term memorisation. Achieving the goal signifies **Success**, and a new topic is introduced and the process **Starts again**. The intention is that every cycle takes the coachee deeper into the language, constantly improving and advancing. One of the most important factors is that the coachee is able to subjectively measure and feel the success of the goals, as this inspires and motivates the coachee to want to learn more.

The imagery behind this process is the movement of a progressive forward-moving spiral. The learner will never come back to the same point once the goals have been achieved; he/she will always come to a point further down the line. If the goals have not been achieved then the movement forward is less, but nevertheless there is a progressive movement forward; there is always some progress.

Here you have the image of the 'spiral learning process':

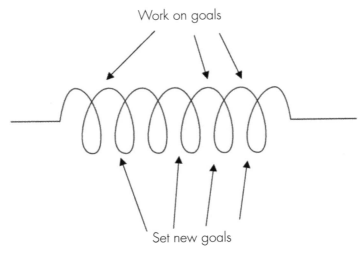

Work on goals

Set new goals

The essential conversations of Neurolanguage Coaching

Neurolanguage Coaching is comprised of three essential conversations – Motivation, Mechanics and Mastery, which I have denominated the 3Ms[72] or the 3 MUSTS. These three conversations are in fact the 3 'musts'!

In an initial session with a new client, there must be an extremely skilled conversation around motivation, there must be an extremely focused mechanical goal-setting and there must be an extremely well-steered mastery goal-setting.

Now, let us take each one of these elements one by one.

Motivation

We have already noted, in the earlier section of this book relating to neuroscience and how the brain likes to learn, that motivation is essential for the learning process. Without motivation, information will not easily be retained in the brain. For this reason, the coach, right at the beginning of the coaching engagement, must have a deep and powerful conversation with the coachee about motivation. There should also be a clear understanding from both sides as to what motivation really means or rather how we interpret the word 'motivation'. What vision does the learner have of speaking fluently? What would perfect English change in his/her life? For example, would it bring a promotion at work? A new job maybe? Enhanced communication with a foreign boyfriend?

We should be aware that the reason for improving the target language may be the same as the motivation to improve; however, it could also be

---

[72] ©Rachel Marie Paling 2012.

totally different. Let me give you an example of this: if I have a client who wants to travel the world, then the reason and motivation for improving the target language could be to speak enough English to be able to travel the world. If I have a client who tells me their reason is to be able to speak more English at work, there could in fact be a motivation which goes beyond that reason, for example, the desire for a promotion or the desire to apply for a better job in an international company. The skilled language coach will be able to ascertain if there is a greater intrinsic motivation lying beyond the 'surface' reasons for learning.

If we think about our 'sports coach' and the mission to motivate the sportsperson to 'win the cup', 'run the fastest' or 'jump the highest/longest', that is exactly what the Neurolanguage coach seeks to find – the intrinsic motivation that is going to inspire and motivate the learner SO MUCH that he/she will want to attend the sessions and even do consolidation out of the sessions to be able to reach their goals and progress even faster and with great impact.

This motivation conversation should be taken in a step-by-step manner, commencing with a motivation diagnostic to find out exactly how motivated the coachee really is, and also what is motivating the coachee to learn or improve the target language.

There can, in fact, be three types of coachee:

1. The 'yes, motivated'
2. The 'not motivated, but there is something in my life which would motivate me to learn the target language'
3. The 'not motivated and nothing in my life which would motivate me to learn the target language'.

1. The 'yes, motivated'

If the coachee clearly has a motivation to learn or improve the target language, the Neurolanguage coach should be able to 'catch' that motivation and get the coachee to hold that vision. Just like the sports coach holds that vision of 'winning the cup' or 'winning the game' or 'breaking a record', the Neurolanguage coach should keep referring back to that vision throughout the language learning process. This serves to inspire, animate and consistently reconnect the learner with his/her chief motivation. It also acts as a 'pick-me-up': whenever the coachee is feeling down or unhappy with progress, the coach can use it to animate and encourage.

For example, I have discovered that my coachee wants to improve so that he will be considered for a promotion. I will check with my client if I can keep reminding him of this and use it as a 'motivating reminder' whenever I can to inspire, animate and keep that vision alive of the client getting that promotion because of his linguistic abilities. Honestly, in my experience, it acts as an instant inspirational 'tonic'.

2. The 'not motivated but there is something . . .'

Many people come to learn a language without really understanding what their deeper intrinsic motivation is to learn it, except for the fact that they want to learn. They have probably never even really thought about what they could do if they spoke the target language fluently and what benefits this could bring to their life. In addition, some people are sent to learn by their company. I personally have had the experience of one company in Germany changing the company lingua franca to English and then forcing their employees to speak and, consequently, to learn it. Obviously, the employees felt this was unfair, and clearly motivation was lacking. In these particular cases, the Neurolanguage coach should skillfully acknowledge and recognise the unfairness of the situation, but at the same time should explain to the coachee that without motivation the brain is possibly not going to learn effectively.

Therefore, the coach must steer the motivation conversation to discover what other areas of the learner's life could benefit from an improved fluency in the target language. What could the learner really achieve in his/her life with that language under their belt? One of my coachees was one such learner and had been forced to improve his English. We circled on motivation and really found nothing that motivated him to learn. Then, we moved into his hobbies and he told me that he was a sailor and sometimes went on sailing holidays. At that moment, his whole energy shifted and he suddenly realised that better English would help him when he was sailing in international waters. When I asked how he would feel if we looked at some sailing language and saw some expressions that actually come into both ordinary and business language like 'learning the ropes', he started to smile and became more interested, motivated and extremely curious. We had tapped into his intrinsic motivation.

Another of my clients told me he would love to help his son with his English, and when I said that was a super idea and we could really focus on getting him able to explain grammar and language areas to his son, he also notably shifted his energy and became very motivated.

Once intrinsic motivation has been found, as in point 1 above, the Neurolanguage coach will know how to take it and keep referring to it throughout the learning process.

3. The 'not motivated and there is nothing . . .'

Finally, we come to the scenario of the 'not motivated learner', who has also not found any benefit from improving the language and no hidden motivation in any other area of his/her life. This is what I would call 'zero motivation'.

The conversation around motivation, at this point, should become extremely honest, and the coach should explain that motivation really is an essential ingredient of the learning process and without it, the learning process will probably not be effective. As no intrinsic motivation has been found, the Neurolanguage coach must steer the conversation to examine the extrinsic or the external factors that could arouse motivation. In other words, what could be motivating about the learning process itself? What activities could be inspiring? How would the coachee like the language sessions to be? What would stimulate the learner to be motivated enough to actually come to those learning sessions every time?

In the end, when lacking intrinsic motives, the process itself becomes the motivation. I have one particular learner who is the perfect example of a 'no motivation to learn English' client. Actually, we touched base on his motivation at the beginning and do this periodically and he recognises that he needs English for work but that he really is not at all motivated to learn it and confesses that he never will be. However, the motivating factor for him is ... me! He confesses he enjoys the sessions we have together, with fascinating conversations, and we always talk about his topics of interest and focus, and he claims his motivation and reason are extrinsically the process that I bring. He has been my client since 2004, though meeting perhaps once a month or every two months, as he has a good C1 level. I have to say I feel quite proud to have kept him connected to the language all these years even as a 'not motivated' client!

Mechanical goal-setting

In the initial session, after ascertaining the real motivation of the learner, the coach should then explain to the learner that the session will be divided into two separate goal-settings: the mechanical goal-setting, which deals with everything to do with the grammar and pronunciation of the language, and the mastery goal-setting, which deals with everything to do with the application of the language, the actual use of the language. Once this has been explained, the conversation should then centre upon finding out the actual level of the learner. Prior to the meeting, a written language level test may be sent to the learner so that the coach can have an idea of the learner's written level according to the Common European Framework, which is one of the standard level indicators in Europe and in other places worldwide. Often a learner has a totally different level for written and spoken language, and the spoken language is often weaker than the written.

Obviously, if the learner has a low level of the target language, most of the initial session will be conducted in the native language and not the target language. It is suggested that if the learner is able to have this initial session in the target language, this will greatly assist the coach to assess the spoken level of the learner.

The coach then initiates the mechanical goal-setting by going into a 'diagnostics' conversation with the learner, so that the coach can hear how the learner speaks, constructs the grammar, uses the vocabulary and the sentence structure. This diagnostics conversation should be conducted in such a way that the learner remains absolutely calm and relaxed, and with no feeling of being tested, but at the same time the coach is skillfully taking the learner through as many different grammatical areas in the shortest time possible. This will mean that the coach must know exactly how the conversation should flow, from present tenses to past tenses to future, to conditional etc., to hear as many different tenses and grammatical constructions as possible and, of course, the pronunciation.

After these 'diagnostics', the coach should then go into a feedback conversation. However, instead of immediately delivering his/her feedback, the coach should firstly ask the coachee how he/she felt with that conversation and how he/she felt with the different grammar areas and if there were any areas that felt better or weaker. Then the coach should ask if there are any grammar areas that the coachee would specifically like to focus in on, so the coachee can choose or highlight problem areas. After this, the coach can then give feedback on what he/she has heard during the diagnostics conversation, highlighting the grammatical difficulties heard, or even highlighting the areas that were avoided to check whether this avoidance was due to lack of knowledge or due to uncertainty. If the coach has noticed a lot of grammar mistakes, it really is at the coach's discretion as to how many of those mistakes he/she should mention. This discretion's purpose is really to take care that the coach does not destroy the confidence of the learner by giving the impression that there were many mistakes. The coach can make a list for him/herself and highlight the most critical areas or the areas that make sense to tackle first, as they could be fundamental areas that need correcting.

At this point, the coachee has given feedback and the coach too, and various grammar areas should have come to light. Now the coachee should be asked which areas he/she would like to set as the first mechanical goals to be worked on. It is recommended to get the coachee to select between one and three mechanical goals, which will later be put together with between one and three mastery goals. This is to ensure that the learner is not overloaded with goals, so that the focus and attention can be brought to just a few select ones.

As mentioned above, the lower the level of the learner, the more the mechanical goal-setting will take place in the native language with just a mini 'diagnostics' conversation to hear any target language knowledge. Obviously, if the learner is a complete beginner then the conversation regarding the mechanical goals centres around how to bring in a step-by-step learning process to block-build the language from scratch. With a beginner, the key is to start with grammar that gets the learner speaking the fastest. For example, in English this would necessarily be the verbs 'to be', 'to have' and the impersonal 'there is' and 'there are', and the formulations of questions and negatives of these. Then it would be a case of step-by-step building the language: introducing present continuous as the real present and the present simple as the facts and habits tense. Clearly, in the case of a beginner the expertise of the Neurolanguage coach will be to steer those initial mechanical goals.

When a learner has a better level, the coach must get the learner to identify the mechanical goals so that the learner really 'owns' those goals. This aspect of ownership is a very important player for the brain. The more that somebody feels that they themselves have set their own goals, the more likely they will be to actually achieve them. 'Specifically, when students set their own goals, they take responsibility and ownership of their learning goals.'[73] It has been found that 'Such goal-directed behavior that results from goal-setting is empowering and proactive'.[74]

---

[73] Turkay, S. (2014) *Setting Goals: Who, Why How?* Manuscript. http://vpal.harvard.edu/publications/setting-goals-who-why-how.

[74] Elliot, A. J., & Fryer, J. W. (2008). *The goal construct*, in Shah, J., and Gardner, W. (eds.) *Handbook of Motivation Science*, pp. 235–250. New York: The Guildford Press.

The mechanical goal-setting process is absolutely essential to establish the grammatical goals that will be focused on at any given time.

Mastery goal-setting

Once the mechanical goals have been set, the conversation then moves into the mastery goal-setting process. This is really about having an in-depth conversation with the learner to find out what exactly he/she wants to use the language for or wants to apply the language to. The coach should steer the conversation from the very general reasons and desired application of the language to much more specific desires, which can then be transformed into specific goals. The coach has to skillfully take the generic area and break it down sufficiently, taking the learner to voice his/her desired goals. For example, let us imagine that our coachee is a lawyer and wants to improve his/her English when speaking with clients. The Neurolanguage coach would then ask questions to pinpoint what exactly the lawyer discusses with clients, what the lawyer feels is the weakest part of the language and what the lawyer thinks is the most important conversation to improve on initially. For example, questions like:

'May I ask you what type of conversations you have with your clients?'

'What area of law do you practise in?'

'So, I'm hearing that you deal with contract law. What parts of that technical language do you feel you would like to improve?'

(Then, just to clarify) 'I understand that you explain contract terms to your clients, you also negotiate contract terms and you mentioned that you draft the contracts. So which of these do you feel you would like to focus in on first?'

'With all that we've talked about, where would you feel you would like to improve first?'

Once the coach has steered the conversation into a broken-down potential list, he/she should ask the coachee to choose which goal or goals he/she would like to set and work on as the first mastery goals.

Next steps after the goal-setting

At this point, the coachee has, in fact, set both mechanical and mastery goals, so the coach should introduce a conversation regarding the 'actions' to work on to achieve those goals. 'Actions' means the active practical steps that the coachee can take towards achieving the goal. This question should be posed to the coachee, who can really decide on what activities he/she would like to perform to achieve the goals. This triggers the concept of ownership, together with the fact that the coachee will normally decide to choose activities that he/she enjoys doing. The coach should note all the activities that the coachee highlights.

There may be learners who really have no idea what activities to do and turn back to the coach and say, 'You are the teacher – you tell me'. In this case, the coach should try and explain to the learner that the idea is to find activities and tasks that the learner enjoys, because we know that the more positive and fun they are for the brain, the more engaged it will be and the more positive chemicals like dopamine will flow and assist making those memories stick. The coach could then make suggestions and ask the coachee to choose the ones that appeal to him/her the most.

During the goal- and action-setting, the most important factor is to empower the coachee to feel that he/she is in the driving seat, driving and setting those desired goals and desired actions to achieve those goals.

Once goals and actions are set, the next question to ask is the time period within which he/she wishes to achieve those goals. For example, there may be two mechanical and two mastery goals with a certain number of actions, and the learner may decide for a period of three months to work on these. This could be considered a reasonable period of time.

If the coachee were to suggest an unrealistic period of time, either too short or excessively long, then the coach should talk this through with the coachee. Obviously, it will also be necessary at this point of time to check with the coachee how many sessions there would be over the time period. Let us imagine the coachee said a period of one month for four goals with only one session per week; then the coach could ask if this could really be achieved in such a short time, checking just how much work the coachee would be prepared to do alone. In the case that the coachee agrees to dedicate substantial time every week on those goals, they might be achieved. However, more often than not when the coach highlights such a short time period, the coachee then readjusts to a more fitting time period.

Should the coachee suggest an extremely long time period in our example above – say one year for four goals – then the coach could suggest having interim reviews at intervals of perhaps one month or two months just to check in with the coachee regarding where the coachee feels that he/she is with regard to each and every one of the goals. This interim check-in normally gives an indication to the coachee of where exactly they are, and it could be that the coachee him or herself realises that the time period set was longer than necessary.

In any case, there should be mini check-ins every so often, or 'pulse checks', just to see where the coachee is with regard to the goals. At the end of the given time period – let us come back to the example of three months – the coach and the coachee should have a goal review conversation. In this conversation, the coach will deal with each goal individually and will check how the coachee feels about each one, whether the coachee feels the goal has been reached, and, if not, what still needs to be done to achieve it. In the event that the goal has been reached, then the question arises as to whether the coachee wants to set a new goal, or a new set of goals. It could be at this point that there is a mix of newly set goals together with perhaps one or two goals that the coachee felt were not yet reached and still wanted to work on.

Just as an after note, the main reason for setting both mechanical goals and mastery goals is to get the learner to apply the language as soon as possible. In the case of a beginner, getting that beginner speaking, even in simple sentences right from the beginning, will boost the motivation and the feeling of achievement and thus inspire the learner to want to learn more. In most cases, there is always a barrier to speaking a language and if we, as Neurolanguage coaches, can help break this barrier down right from the start, then we will be nurturing a confident speaker who is then encouraged to come into the performing and doing brain rather than the thinking brain.

Obviously, the coach is the language expert and, in some ways, the mechanical goals may be steered by the coach a little bit, in the sense that, yes, the coachee will be saying what they would prefer to work on but the coach will also, from time to time, be introducing totally new grammar areas to bring the coachee further and deeper into the language. With an extremely advanced learner, there may actually be less focus on grammatical areas and more emphasis on the actual application of the language. In fact, extremely advanced learners are sometimes quite difficult to deal with because they have often reached a place of complacency and just want to maintain the language. I often find that in these cases it is interesting to stimulate the advanced speaker to want to dive even deeper into greater fluency, greater native expressions and really go deep into complex grammar areas, such as ellipsis and inversions in English.

So, we have seen how the 3Ms really are the backbone conversations of the Neurolanguage Coaching process.

Giving structure and form to a Neurolanguage Coaching engagement

To achieve the art of Neurolanguage Coaching there has to be an ongoing flow through a structured engagement. This structure is given through five core parts of the Neurolanguage Coaching process denominated the 5Cs.[75]

These five core parts are comprised of:

1. Concrete requirements
2. Clear targets and commitment
3. Coaching conversation throughout
4. Connecting the brain and conquering barriers
5. Completion of goals

1. Concrete requirements

Above all, a Neurolanguage coach must meet the ethical guidelines and professional standards related to coaching and to the International Coach Federation (ICF) programme accreditation. This corresponds to the ICF competence 1, meeting ethical guidelines and professional standards. This naturally imports the appropriate professional conduct with clients and of course includes confidentiality and privacy. Clearly, one of the first steps will be to make the contract with the client regarding the engagement, to be signed by both parties (which corresponds to the ICF competence 2). It is also essential for the Neurolanguage coach to establish trust and intimacy right from the start (ICF competence 3). In this way, the coach creates a safe, supportive environment that produces ongoing mutual respect and

---

[75] © Rachel Marie Paling 2012.

trust in the sessions. This should be continuously demonstrated through personal integrity, honesty and sincerity, demonstrating respect at all times for the client's perception, learning style and unique way of learning.

After the formalities have been established, the coach should check what the coachee actually knows about Neurolanguage Coaching, giving a full explanation about the process if the coachee has no idea.

The next stage would be to explore the motivation. As we saw above, motivation has to be addressed and ascertained right at the beginning of the process.

A written level test may be sent to the learner prior to the initial session and would provide insight into the current level of understanding. In the first session, this level test can be discussed, highlighting, from both sides, the areas that were stronger or weaker. The most important 'test' should be the spoken diagnostics, which the coach conducts in person with the coachee in this initial session. I also mentioned previously the importance of how to go through the feedback with the learner and also how the learner should be absolutely interactive in the whole discussion.

2. Clear targets and commitment

Having completed the diagnostics, there should be a clear decision from the learner regarding the mechanical goals or the goals to work on related to grammar. Throughout the feedback and goal-setting there will be continuous active listening (ICF competence 5), powerful questions (ICF competence 6) and direct communication (ICF competence 7). The coach will also be constantly creating awareness (ICF competence 8).

Regarding the mastery side of the language, the coach will then move into a coaching conversation following the funnelling down principal, from generic to specific, to find out exactly what the learner would like to set as the concrete mastery goals for advancing in the target language. The goal-setting falls under ICF competence number 10, and in addition, after the goal-setting, there will be a skilled conversation to get the learner to design his/her actions (ICF competence 9).

Both goal-setting processes will require strong coaching presence as well (ICF competence 4). There should be commitment from the coach and coachee, with a definite time period set by the learner and desired frequency of sessions. Both parties become accountable and, in addition, the language coach will be responsible for managing the progress (ICF competence 11).

At this point, the Neurolanguage coach has all the essential ingredients to craft and design the path forward, creating a suggested agenda which skillfully factors in all of the learner's desired goals and all of his/her desired actions over the chosen time period, carefully ensuring that material is repeated and revisited to facilitate long-term memory 'wiring'. This suggested agenda could be only for the first half of the chosen time period and sent to the learner for approval. Then at the halfway mark of the time period, there could be a touch-base conversation, checking how the learner feels about the progress and the goals themselves, and from this conversation the second half of the agenda could be mapped out and sent to the coachee for approval.

3. Coaching conversation throughout

Once the mechanical and mastery goals have been set, the time period and session frequency agreed and the suggested agenda crafted, then the actual language coaching sessions begin. These ongoing sessions are indeed active coaching conversations with great focus and attention on the goals and actions, working to achieve the desired goals. The predominance of quiet, brain-friendly coaching conversations, in a non-directive and non-demonstrative style, will always ensure an extremely calm and tranquil limbic system. This in turn potentially creates a better learning process and steers the learner more and more into the performing brain. The Neurolanguage coach will constantly be trying to mitigate the threat status and create the positive ideal learning state. There will be a fluid interplay of active listening and powerful questioning, whereby the coach establishes a balance between the fine art of block-building and correcting grammatical mechanical issues as well as reinforcing the mastery 'application' of the target language.

So, coaching conversations are absolutely endemic to the language learning process.

4. Connecting the brain and conquering barriers

The principles of neuroscience pervade the whole process. The Neurolanguage coach is consistently the 'provocateur par excellence' to stimulate brain associations. So, the coach becomes the omnipresent facilitator for the coachee's work of connecting and associating. In addition, there should be a constant awareness of emotional blocks or any other barriers that could be triggering the threat response of the limbic system, which in turn could cause limited resources in the 'learning areas' of the brain. There could be a number of barriers that affect the learning process – emotional, cultural, status related, motivational, physical, relating to corporate environments, comprehension issues to name just a few. Language learning can be an extremely embarrassing experience and, as we know, confidence and certainty are really major issues for anyone learning a language. It is the role of the Neurolanguage coach to make the client feel safe and secure in making mistakes, and even to assist the client to forget that he/she is speaking in a different language.

As the language coach has to always be on his/her toes between mechanical goals and mastery goals there has to be a continuous flow of significant positive feedback; asking the right questions; keeping the client in tune with his/her emotions about learning; introducing new topics; practising the topics; consolidating and asking permission. It is a never-ending dance of language and coaching with a constant interaction between both. The coachee should always be stretched with exactly the right questions and situations to make him/her think about the language, about the grammar and how it compares to the native language, trigger words, expressions, etc.

Another type of barrier could relate to a cultural use of the target language, as often culture and language go hand-in-hand. It really is an added bonus to language coaching when the coach has detailed knowledge and experience of the culture of the target language country and throughout the coaching conversations the coach can often convey the reason for some things to be said in the manner that they are said – for example, the use of understatement in British English or the very direct manner of German.

There is a definite feeling with today's pervasive neuroscience that Neurolanguage Coaching is creating much more awareness (ICF competence 8) and really allows the coachee to understand the rationale behind certain behaviour, expressions or structures and in this way allows him/her to relate or connect better through an associative learning process.

Here is a summary of how to achieve constant brain connections:

- Chunk material down
- Utilise constant repetition from both coach and coachee
- Formulate and reformulate
- Check how your coachee learns best – what type of learner is he/she?
- Questions formulated with emotion and motivation
- Grab the full attention of the coachee
- Aim for a goal-focused state to catch attention and provide motivation
- Make it 'real' and 'personal' and therefore relevant
- Change learning techniques constantly
- Use humour
- Keep the material interesting and novel
- Carry out language coaching through storytelling or through social issues
- Make learning easy to digest with order and structure
- Include visualisations
- Ask the coachee to evaluate the meaning of the new language aspect being learnt and compare it to his/her own language

- Ask the coachee to contextualise the information and then to apply it
- Ask the coachee to use the language learnt by relating a personal experience, or ask him/her to then formulate the information in a different way
- Ask ongoing questions to trigger a recovery of learning content and enable more associations of the learning content
- Ask the right questions to get the coachee thinking more and associating
- Ask the coachee to visualise the grammar or language learnt
- Check with the coachee when to give feedback about errors – immediately when he/she makes a mistake or after a sentence or a paragraph?
- Ensure that the language coaching is active, not boring, and whenever possible positive, and even fun
- Acknowledge the coachee as frequently as possible to create the positive feeling around the learning and give recognition that the coachee is making progress
- Space out testing/consolidation of vocabulary
- Revisit learning material within a certain period of time to enable the retrieval of information and the enhancement of long-term memory
- Establish trust and intimacy with the client
- Instil coachee with confidence
- Provide the coachee with a safe environment
- Always be aware of social pain issues/scenarios
- Try to discover emotional issues and use coaching conversations to assist the coachee through them
- Share your cultural experiences with the coachee if you lived in the target language country
- Explain style and manner of speech so that the coachee can understand cultural implications – in particular formal and informal language structures inherent to the language such as the 'polite you' forms in many languages.

5. Completion of goals

When the chosen time period comes to an end, both Neurolanguage coach and coachee should hold a review of the goals and ascertain whether the goals have been reached and how the coachee feels about them. If the coachee feels they have indeed reached the goals, then the next step would be to initiate a new goal-setting process for both mechanical and mastery goals. If, however, the coachee feels that the goals, or some of the goals, have not yet been reached, the coach should explore whether the coachee would like to work further on these goals and, if so, for how long. The coach should also check if there may be some other actions that the coachee would prefer to engage in at this point and/or repeat actions that he/she had chosen previously. The coachee may wish to identify new goals to work on through a new mechanical and/or mastery goal-setting process.

As already explained above, the continual flow of setting goals, working towards these, then achieving them, reflects a spiral progressive learning process.

The learner may, after a period of time, decide to cease the engagement completely, and the coach could then conduct a final review of the goals and go through a feedback form to obtain an idea of the impact of the language coaching process on the learner.

We have now seen how the 5Cs lay down the structure for the Neurolanguage Coaching process. Accompanying this process, there should be adequate administration of the engagement. This should be reflected in forms that illustrate the mechanical goals, the mastery goals, the chosen actions, the time period and frequency, the individual sessions and the goal reviews. These forms will ensure that the entire process is extremely well documented and can serve as a record not only for the learner but also for the Neurolanguage coach to firmly keep track of where the learner is at any given time. The goal sheet forms may even be signed by both coach and coachee to really imprint the intention and the commitment of both parties to the entire process.

With the necessary documentation, and in particular with the goal review sheets, there will be a constant measurement of success and hopefully a constant feeling of achievement. Measuring success in language learning is extremely difficult in practice, as the normal way to measure success has always been and still is the written test, which nowadays is mostly a multiple-choice. Often, learners struggle the most with the spoken side of a language, which, obviously, is the most essential part! The goal review and the continual focus on the spoken language in every single coaching session allows the learner to come into a subjective measurement of success. The more a learner feels that they are able to speak the language, the more motivated and inspired they will be to learn more.

The language learning process could be described as a step learning process, like a staircase, but not just a flight of normal steps! It really reflects those long tread steps which have a longer plateau than normal and then a short step up. This staircase represents the feeling of no progress for such a long time and feeling stuck on a long plateau. Then, suddenly, we take a small step up and we start to feel that we understand more, we can speak more and we generally feel a difference. However, then it happens again: that feeling of 'nothing happening' and 'no improvement' and, again, we find ourselves on the next long plateau – feeling despondent and depressed because we feel no progress – when suddenly, we go up another small step, and so on, and so on. This is the 'long tread, short rise' stairway to fluency, and achieving those goals along the way is the real reflection of that small step upwards that we take each time we improve.

Long tread staircase, Sitges, Barcelona

Part V

Delivering grammar though brain-friendly coaching conversations

The most prominent skill of the Neurolanguage coach is the delivery of ANY grammatical topic through what can only be described as an extremely quiet, brain-friendly coaching conversation. In this way, the coach avoids any negative threat response from the coachee and, in addition, enables and facilitates immediate connections and associations, as well as the instant application of the grammar in spoken language.

PACT PQC© is a model which I have created and which lays down the pathway for the coach to conduct such quiet conversations. The essence of the model is to direct the brain through focused, directed conversations, stretching the learner beyond their current knowledge, consolidating what is already known, introducing new material wherever necessary and provoking new connections.[76]

The model stands for:

P – Placement

A – Assessment

C – Conversation

T – Teach

PQ – Powerful Questions

C – Clarification

---

[76] ©Rachel Marie Paling 2013.

Yet, the model itself may not be linear, and the ability and flexibility of the coach to come in and out of the various parts of the model will allow the coaching conversation to adapt to the dynamic of the learner sitting in front of the coach at any given time (remembering that no two brains are the same!). The model may commence in the order in which it is given, but then any of the parts may be used according to how the coach sees fit. This will depend entirely on the expertise of the coach, in relation to how he/she is able to break down the grammatical topic to build it back up step-by-step throughout the conversation, as well as the ability of the coach to adapt to the learner by actively listening and posing powerful questions.

Now let us look at each of these parts of the model individually.

P – Placement

Placement means signposting language. It is one of the terms that David Rock uses in his Dance of Insight coaching model.[77] As language trainers, I think a lot of us have the experience of assisting learners with the delivery of presentations in a foreign language, and most of us have the experience of delivering presentations in our native language. If you can imagine the signposting language which is given when we deliver presentations, the idea is to constantly connect the audience to what is being presented. This is exactly the same type of signposting that this particular model commands. It is absolutely essential to indicate exactly what part of the grammar we are talking about at any given time, and the coach must have a clear map of where he/she is and where he/she is taking that particular grammar conversation and must clearly signal this map all along the way. This means that both the coach and the coachee will constantly be at the same point in the conversation and the attention of the coachee will be maximised. One of the ladies who took my course called this 'GPS mapping', and what a superb way of describing it.

---

[77] Rock, D. (2007) *Quiet Leadership: Six Steps to Transforming Performance at Work.* New York: HarperBusiness.

Examples of placement could be:

'Well, in this session we are going to come in and focus on your first goal, which is "to feel more confidence when using the present tenses". How does that sound to you?'

'Firstly let us begin with the present continuous ...'

'Now, how about we focus on the actual formation of the present continuous?'

'Super, now we have in fact covered the formation and you have done really well and now we're going to move on to how we formulate questions in the present continuous.'

'Well done, your questions are sounding really good and now let's move the focus into the negative form of the present continuous.'

Signposting or 'placement' shows that there is a constant thread running through the conversation. Obviously, it is an invisible thread that the coach is very much in charge of steering and, as we said, the main purpose is to keep both coach and coachee on the same track at the same time.

A – Assessment

The next step after introducing and placing the grammatical topic is to thoroughly explore and assess what the coachee already knows about this topic. This is because, as the coach, we need to understand and find out exactly where the coachee is with his/her understanding and ability to express what he/she knows. This will indicate to you exactly how much the coachee knows, highlight potential misunderstandings or lack of knowledge and may indicate where mistakes are coming from. It will also allow you to hear mistakes relating to formation and finally, it will highlight confusion. You could also include in this assessment a question relating to how this particular grammar area compares to the same grammar area in the native language, just to hear how the learner relates and associates (or not) the target language grammar area with the native language area.

More often than not, we never really explore what our learner already knows, and, in fact, it could be that our learner actually knows more than we thought, so in this way we ascertain already acquired knowledge, and we avoid any repetitions that could lead to our learner feeling bored or frustrated because they are repeating areas they already know. Once the coach realises that the learner knows a certain part of the grammar, there is no need to go into it and the coach can swiftly move into other grammar parts.

Examples of assessment could be:

'Now, could I ask you to tell me what you know about the present tenses in English?'

'May I ask you how we form the present in English?'

'Could I just ask, firstly, how many present tenses are there? Super, can you tell me which they are?'

'Now, I hear you say that we have two presents in English, the continuous and the simple ... would you be able to tell me how we form these tenses?'

'How about the negative form of that tense – how is it formed?'

'And could you tell me about the question form? How do we make it?'

C – Conversation

After each assessment of a grammatical area, the coach engages the coachee in a practice conversation concerning the real life and personal situations of the coachee to get him/her to practise the grammatical area that is being explored. This action gets the coachee to connect with the explanations and implement the focused grammar, getting the learner to apply the grammar instantly. This should bring enough attention into the prefrontal cortex and the hippocampus to start generating the 'brain connections'.

Mini conversations may be introduced at various intervals. There could be some conversation after the **Assessment** part of PACT to check if the coachee is implementing the language correctly, or conversation could occur after **Teach**, so the learner is instantly applying newly acquired knowledge and testing it out. So, these mini conversations serve the purpose of confirming what the learner already knows, or immediately applying newly acquired information.

Examples of language to introduce conversations could be:

'Thank you for telling me about the present continuous. Now, let us put this into practice a little bit. Could you tell me what you are doing at the moment? What about your family, what are they doing?'

'And now let us move on to practise the present simple: may I ask you to tell me what you normally do on a Monday? What about at the weekends?'

'Now, we have just been looking at the formation of questions, so how about you ask me as many questions as you like?'

T – Teach

There will be times when the coachee demonstrates a lack of knowledge or confusion regarding a grammatical area. Language coaching then becomes a dance between language teaching and language coaching and at this point the Neurolanguage coach must use his/her expertise as a teacher and introduce new grammar. However, whenever new material is introduced the coaching style will ensure that it is not delivered in the traditional directive teaching style. This means a non-directive, quiet, brain-friendly coaching style will prevail, ensuring that the learner's limbic system remains calm at all times and thus open to receive and directly apply new knowledge. As mentioned above, the **Teach** part of this model will only be necessary wherever there is a deficit in the knowledge of the learner or where a totally new grammatical topic is being explored.

Examples of **Teach** could be:

'Thank you for that excellent conversation on the present tenses – now we have, in fact, discovered that there are some verbs that never take the continuous form in the present. How about if we introduce this particular grammar point and focus on this now?'

'So, we now know that there are in fact some verbs that never take the "continuous form" – could you perhaps brainstorm some of these for me?'

'Well done, and yes, the verbs "to love" and "to hate" or "to dislike" are examples of these verbs. Now may I just give you some more, and how about if we get them into categories so that you can relate to them better? For example, we could create a category of "emotional" verbs, as you already mentioned love, hate, dislike. Maybe we could also add "to like", "to need", "to deserve", "to prefer" – these are what we call "state" verbs as opposed to "action" verbs. Now, how about we try to use these in some sentences?'

'You have superbly dealt with the state and action verbs. Thank you for that. I would like to go one step further now, if I may. There are, in fact, some verbs that can be both action and state verbs – were you aware of that? Okay, so I'm hearing that is new for you. How about if we explore some examples together. First, let's take the verb "to weigh". Now, can you tell me when I would say "I am weighing something" and when I would say "it weighs"?

'What would you say is the difference between using the continuous form and using the simple form?'

Interwoven with the PACT part of the model at all times is the PQC aspect – **Powerful Questions** and **Clarification**.

PQ – Powerful Questions

These should be used at all times, not only as stimulants and encouragements for the topics and conversations but also as provocations for brain connections/associations and disconnections/disassociations.

Examples of **Powerful Questions** relating to language and grammar could be:

'May I ask you to try to think of the French/Italian/Spanish/German word and see if you can connect to the word in English?'

'How similar is this grammatical issue to the same issue in your language?'

'How could you build a connecting bridge to this word to help you remember it?'

'Let us connect the tenses to your language – how similar are these tenses to the tenses in your language?'

'How is that said in your own language?'

'What differences are there between this and your own language?'

'What similarities are there between this and your own language?'

'I notice that you said XXX; could it be that this is similar to your own language?'

'Let us try and understand where this mistake is coming from.'

'How can we disconnect this word so that you do not think of the German word when you see it?'

'How could you say that in a different way?'

'What is another word which means exactly the same as that word?'

'What is the opposite of that word?'

'Can you give me alternatives to that word – maybe three or four?'

C – Clarification

Clarification should always be used to really consolidate what the learner is saying and to clarify what he/she means. This brings clarity to any confusion or misunderstanding or lack of knowledge wherever necessary. As coaches, we often reformulate what we hear in different words, so that the coachee may hear back what they had said in a different way. This allows the coachee to verify what they said and, in addition, it brings in a new set of vocabulary and expressions, which enrichens the learning process, allowing the learner to hear, learn and associate new variations of the language.

Examples of **Clarification** could be:

'Am I hearing that ...?'

'So, what you are saying is that ...'

'In other words, you mean ...'

'So, that is to say ...'

'Am I right in thinking that you mean ...?'

'Ah, that means ...'

'If I say this in another way, then ...'

'Let me put this in a different way. In fact, I am hearing that ...'

'That sounds like ...'

In essence, the PACT PQC model will allow the Neurolanguage coach to perform a dance between coaching and teaching through any grammatical topic in a quiet and extremely enjoyable coaching conversation. The skilled coach will come in and out of all of those parts of the model to really maximise the conversation and connect directly and quickly with the grammar in such a way that there is an instant application and comprehension.

Behind this model, the Neurolanguage coach is an absolute expert at chunking down any grammar topic. We now know and comprehend that by chunking grammar down into bite-size pieces, the brain will be able to deal better with this step-by-step build-up of language.

If we take an example of how to break down a grammar topic, let us first look at breaking down the present tenses and then building them up step-by-step and purposefully, following a particular pattern so that the brain can create built-in pathways to assist making the necessary neural connections relating to this topic.

Present tenses breakdown

(a) Introduce the present continuous tense:

- Formation – to be + ING
- Introduce the question form
- Introduce the negative form
- When is it used?
- Introduce the trigger words/indicators to show that the present continuous should be used

(b) Introduce the present simple:

- Formation
- Care to be taken with the he/she/it endings
- Spelling rules for the S or ES endings?
- Introduce the question form – verb DO/DOES
- Introduce the negative form – verb DO/DOES
- When is it used?
- Introduce the trigger words/indicators to show that the present simple should be used – brainstorm a list of these words

(c) Compare/contrast present continuous and present simple in easy contrasting sentences.

(d) Introduce state and action verbs:

- discuss the differences between these types of verbs
- brainstorm a list of state verbs and categorise wherever possible
- brainstorm a list of verbs which can be both, but with passive/active feel e.g. – 'to weigh'

- brainstorm a list of verbs which can be both, but then which have different meanings according to the tense, e.g. 'to see': 'I see a dog' vs. 'I am seeing my friend this evening'

(e) Introduce the idea that both present simple and present continuous may also be used as future tenses.

- present simple as a future
- present continuous future

Example of PACT PQC in action

Background information: Roger is a B2/C1 English speaker (Spanish is his native language). He is quite fluent but there are some recurring mistakes in the present tenses.

Roger, we had talked about your goals in our initial session and one of your mechanical goals is in fact to really consolidate your present tenses in English, so that you feel much more confident and the differences between the two tenses become more automatic language for you. How would you feel if we pick up this particular goal in this session today and explore a little bit? (P)

> That sounds good. You know I have quite a few problems with the differences between the present tenses. So yes, that would be good to come a little bit more into this.

Great. Now, I suggest that we start right from the beginning. I know that you are extremely fluent and definitely you know a lot about the present tenses, but I suggest we take it step-by-step and build it up so that we can really identify where it is you have some confusion or maybe even things that you had not realised before. Is that okay with you? (P)

> Yes that sounds interesting.

Super. Then, Roger, what can you tell me about the present tenses in English? (A)

> Okay well that I know that there are two ways to express the present in English. One is the progressive and the other is the simple. I know that the progressive is the ING ending and this is similar to the Spanish that we have, I mean the ANDO and the IENDO endings, and the other is just the simple form of the verb, like 'I eat'.

Excellent, well done. Yes, you are right, we have the present progressive or the present continuous and we have the present simple. (Clar.) Now, how about we take each one of those separately and we just go through the formation, the use and the words that indicate to us that we are in fact in one of those tenses. So, let's just take the present progressive at the moment and focus in on this. (P) You mentioned the formation, so what in fact are the elements that form the present progressive? (A)

Well, we take the verb 'to be' and then we take the verb with the ending ING. 'I am eating', 'I am drinking' or 'I am thinking'.

Okay. You mentioned before that the ING ending is similar to the Spanish gerund ending, so may I ask do you also form the present progressive with the verb 'to be' in Spanish? (PQ)

Yes, you're right. We do, we say 'Estoy comiendo, estoy bebiendo' and we use the verb 'Estar' in Spanish.

And may I ask you, do you use this present progressive in Spanish in the same way that we use it in English? (PQ)(A)

You know, I never really thought of it like this, but yes, we do. We use it for something that we are doing now and I think this is exactly the same in English. We use this for what we are doing now, so 'I am eating' means in this moment.

Yes, well done. So, I'm hearing that you understand the formation and generally when we use it. May I just ask you to bring it into a bit of a conversation with me, using the affirmative, the question and the negative, just so that I can hear that you're using it in the right way? (C)

Yes, sure. Well, I'm talking with you right now and we are discussing the present tenses. I'm not eating anything and you are not drinking anything. I'm thinking hard what to say and I'm not feeling very concentrated. Are you listening to me?

(More conversation would be elicited by the coach)

Well done. That was super. You are definitely using it well, and, just as a final question regarding this tense, you have mentioned the word 'now' to indicate that you are in this tense. What other key indicator words could you use? (A)

Okay, so you mean at the moment or currently or in these moments?

Yes absolutely. In fact, all the expressions that bring in that feeling of now, I like to express it like a window of time reflecting now, so this could mean this week, this month even this year. (T)(Clar.) So, could you give me some examples using that sort of wider window of now? (C)

Yes. This week I am working a lot. This month I'm not eating a lot. This year I'm travelling a lot.

Great. Are you feeling okay with the present progressive and all that we've spoken about? (PQ)

Yes, I'm feeling fine. I really can understand that there is quite a parallel to the Spanish formation and also the use.

Well done. Now, let's move away from the progressive and let's turn towards the present simple. (P) You mentioned that we use the simple form of the verb, so that is the infinitive without the 'to', and how about you give me some examples of the present simple? (C)

Ok. I eat, I sleep, I walk to work, I arrive at the office at 7.00am.

Great. Now I just want to check with you about the endings for he/she/it. What is unusual about these endings? (A)(PQ)

Oh yes of course, 'S' is added so, he eats, she sleeps, it drinks some water.

Excellent. Can I just check with you if you are okay with the spelling rules – I mean when we add 'S' and when we add 'ES'? (Clar.)

Yes, I think I am okay with that. I believe that the words ending with S, SH, CH, X and SS take the 'ES' ending. So, I am quite okay with that.

Now may I just quickly move into the question and the negative? How do we form these? (A)

Well, the question is with 'do' or 'does', and the negative 'don't' and 'doesn't'.

Super, I can really hear that you are fine with these. How about we have a small conversation just to get them into practice and hear if in fact the present simple is in place in the conversation? (C)

Okay.

So, Roger, can you just take me through your weekly routine and also just check in with me about my routine too? (C)

Okay. Well, I work every week from Monday to Friday, but sometimes I also work at the weekend. I am working in an energy company. We focus on renewable energy and I work in the wind energy sector.

So, Roger I am hearing that you are working in an energy company and in fact you mentioned this with the present continuous. As a listener, what is the feeling that you think I get when you tell me that you are working in a company and not that you work? (PQ)

Ah, so I should say 'I work', because that is where I always work?

Exactly. If you tell me I am working ... then it gives me the feeling that you are there in a temporary position or a temporary job. (T) Okay, now how about you ask me some questions in the present simple? (A)

Where do you work?

Actually, I work for myself. I am a language coach and have my own private clients.

Do you like it?

Yes, I do.

How often do you work?

Well, I really work every day, like you, and sometimes at the weekends. I don't work on Sundays and I hope you don't work on Sundays either.

No I don't. I really relax on Sunday.

(Then more conversation would be elicited by the coach)

Okay, Roger. Well done. I can hear that the present simple comes quite naturally, in the affirmative, question and also the negative. Now, can you just confirm to me when we actually use the present simple? (A)

When we do something all the time or often, for example.

Yes, super. So, when we want to express a habit and this can be in the affirmative and also in the negative, so 'I don't often go to the cinema', for example. (T) Now, out of curiosity, in this the same in Spanish? (PQ)

Well, actually, if I think about it, you know, in Spanish I can use 'como' for 'I eat' or for 'I am eating', so we use our present indicative for both. Although if I really want to emphasise that I am doing something in the moment, then I would use the 'estoy comiendo'. That is interesting. I had not really thought about it before!

So I am hearing that it is slightly different, then, in Spanish. (Clar.) I agree that it is interesting and a good observation from you. Okay. You remember in the present continuous we spoke about the words that indicate to me that I am in that time, so which are the key indicators or the trigger words for the present simple? (A)

I can think of often, sometimes, never, always, usually ... mmmmm, every day, every month etc., on Sundays.

Excellent. Well done, quite a few there. May I hint a few more in Spanish and see if you connect them to the English words? Like normalmente o raramente? (PQ)

Ah, normally, rarely, also seldom . . .

Well done. That's super. So, these words really indicate that you are in the present simple. Now, how about you just give me some examples that contrast the simple with the continuous? For example, 'I normally go to the office by car, but this morning I am taking the train.' (C)

Okay. I am eating some chocolate, but normally I never eat chocolate. I am also drinking some coffee, but I often drink tea.

(More examples would be given)

Great. Now I have a question for you. We have gone through the present continuous and the present simple, and I am hearing that you are fine with both. (P) Now, are you aware that there are some verbs in English that never go into a continuous form? (PQ) (A)

Mmmm, I am not sure what you mean.

May I explain a little more? There are some verbs that never take the ING ending – they are always used in the simple form. We call them the state verbs, they reflect a state of being or feeling, so what I mean is that they are not actions. (T)

Oh, I understand. Yes, for example, I know, I understand.

Exactly, that is exactly what I mean. How about we bring these into some categories or families to just check that you know the main ones? Maybe we could take the verbs that express emotions first. (A)

Let me think ... I love, I like, I hate, I dislike ... I prefer also maybe?

Super, now what about the verbs that involve the brain? (A)

You mean, I understand, I know, I realise, I believe, I mean ...

Great. Now what about verbs like have or hold? (A)

Yes, to have, definitely. Also to own, to possess, to hold, to contain, to consist of ...

Super. So, we have various categories there for you to remember these verbs. How do you feel with them? (PQ)

I think okay.

Shall we just have a quick conversation to practise some of these verbs? Are you okay to just go through the verbs and the categories and give me some examples using each and connecting with things in your life? (C)

Okay. Well, I know my wife likes different things to me. I hate tea and she loves it. I enjoy walking in the rain, but she doesn't like it. I understand that she believes in good things, so she seems to be an optimist. We own a little house and we have three children and a dog. The house consists of seven rooms and there is a little garden.

(More conversation would be elicited by the coach)

Excellent. Well done. Are you feeling okay with those? (PQ)

Yes, okay. But I know there are some verbs which I am confused with. Some verbs can be both but they have a different meaning. For example, to see or to hold.

Yes, you are absolutely right. Normally, we can use these verbs in both the present simple or the present continuous. You are right that the meaning can change. So, when will I use I see? And when would I use I'm seeing? (A)

Well, I would say I see the girl playing over there or I would say tomorrow I am seeing my mother, so in the second example it means I am visiting her. Is that right?

Yes, it is. What about to hold? (A)

The bottle holds five litres, or I am holding the baby.

Well done. How about we brainstorm and make a list of some of these verbs? (A)

(The coach and coachee then proceed to create a list of verbs that take different meanings in the two present tenses)

(The coach would then proceed to put these into practice and get them into a conversation)

Now, Roger, so far we have gone through both the present continuous and the present simple. We have gone through the formation of both, the use, the trigger words and we have compared the two tenses. Then we talked about state verbs and we have brainstormed and categorised some of those verbs that never take the ING ending. We then brainstormed the verbs that take different meanings in both the present tenses and we have practised these as well. (P) How do you feel about the present tenses now? (PQ)

I'm feeling okay. I feel that I have clarified some doubts and it has helped me become more clear with both and I feel that now it's about getting them into conversation and really making sure that I have them in the right place.

Yes, and we can make sure that we do that over the next weeks, just to consolidate everything that we have gone through. Now, as a final thought, could we just explore another use of the present tenses? Which use of the present tenses have we not talked about? (A)

Both present tenses can be used for the future, I believe?

Excellent. Could you tell me a little bit more about them? (A)

Well, I know that the present continuous is for something that is very near in the future, so I can say I am visiting my mother this evening. I think it is also for something that is planned, so I am definitely visiting her. But I am not sure about when I would use the present simple.

Well done. You are right about the present continuous in the future, and may I give you some sentences in Spanish and then you translate them into English for me? (A) (PQ)

Okay.

117

El tren llega luego a las tres. El avión aterriza a las 20.00 de la noche.

> Oh, I see. The train arrives later at three and the aeroplane lands at eight o'clock this evening. So, we use this present simple for timetables and schedules. Don't we?

Yes, we do. That is excellent, because I'm hearing that you understand how to use both the present tenses as future indicators. That means we have more or less covered everything to do with the present tenses and with pleasure we can consolidate and really make sure that you feel more and more confident with them and when to use each of them. (Clar.) We are going to finalise the session now (P) and just as the final question, may I ask you, what could you do between now and our next session that could help you really think about these two present tenses and maybe do some consolidation work alone? (PQ)

> Good question. I think I would like to go through what we did and especially the lists and brainstorming that we did. Maybe I could create a little written paragraph every day of things that I am doing and contrast this with my normal routines of the day. Almost like a little diary. That could be interesting!

Well, it really sounds like a great idea. I look forward to you telling me what you've written next week when we meet. How do you feel about today's conversation? (PQ)

> Actually, it was very good because it made me think a lot about the Spanish and English and it also helped me to clarify a lot, especially where I had some doubts. It was also a nice, easy conversation so I didn't feel like we were talking about grammar. And I'm also looking forward to next week's session. Thank you.

Thank you too, Roger. And I would like to say that you have excellent English and all we are doing is really just getting it even more perfect and helping you to lose those little mistakes. Well done!

(Note from the author: each grammar conversation flows with its own dynamic and according to each individual learner. In some parts of the above conversation, there would be more interchange and conversation, which for the purposes of this book has been shortened and adapted to demonstrate the PACT PQC model in practice. Obviously, the lower the level of the learner, the fewer areas of the present tenses topic would be covered.)

We have seen how the PACT PQC model can be used as the backbone for a coaching conversation around any grammatical topic. We should take into account that, in fact, the model could be used for any grammar area; all it needs is the skilled breakdown by the coach prior to the session with the coachee. Then this breakdown is steered through the PACT PQC conversation which moves from the constant signposting, to the continuous assessment of what the learner already knows, to the consistent application and conversation and, whenever necessary, the introduction of new information through a non-directive, brain-friendly style. Powerful questions are inherent in any coaching process as well as clarifications/reformulations.

By moving grammar into brain-friendly coaching conversations, I have found (and so have the trainers who have certified with me) that the learner remains calmer, feels more empowered to understand and apply it and even starts to enjoy talking about grammar. I would always recommend introducing grammar in this way and not from books. Books can be used as a next step for self-consolidation and self-study, but grammar should be brought alive and applied instantly.

Final word from the author:
The way forward

Over the past three years, just over 150 language teachers have taken the Neurolanguage Coaching certification course to become certified and accredited Neurolanguage coaches. I am extremely grateful to the first groups of people who trusted in this certification programme and really took on board the philosophy and the message which this programme brings, and now more and more language teachers are interested and curious about how to change their style of delivery and the whole language learning process.

We live in an increasingly globalised world, and somehow we need to inspire not only children but also adults, whether from the private sphere or the corporate world, to learn more languages and to come into a better communication with each other worldwide and on all levels. It is not enough to think that English is the predominant language in the world; it should also be commonplace for English natives to learn other languages, and I sincerely admire people who *do* master another language, or languages. I myself have been lucky enough to acquire French, Spanish, Italian, German as well as some Catalan, basic Russian and basic Arabic. I am just embarking on Mandarin Chinese, and I would love over the next years to really master Russian, Arabic and Mandarin Chinese, even coming into Japanese. I would like to think that by the time I am 80 years old I can speak ten languages or more.

My whole philosophy behind Neurolanguage Coaching touches upon the question of how we, as educators, can take the principles of neuroscience and coaching to enhance the learning process and to help our learners to learn better, faster and more efficiently with a brain-friendly coaching style. Through Neurolanguage Coaching we also build up our awareness of the impact, both negative and positive, we can have on a learner, and how we can fully empower the learner to succeed, moving the learner away from threat responses and limbic reactions that hinder and block the brain from learning effectively.

I have also just created a programme to deliver Neurolanguage Communication training to teachers of any discipline, assisting them in their transition from directive school 'teacher' style to a brain-friendly, non-directive 'coaching' style.

In some ways, my approach and style could be seen to echo the provocation of thoughts which the Socratic debate evoked. In the Socratic approach, there was a form of cooperative argumentative dialogue based on asking and answering questions to stimulate critical thinking and to draw out ideas and underlying presumptions. Nowadays, there are certain schools which also aim to develop critical reasoning; for example, Waldorf education is based on this as well as empathic understanding, with the aim of developing free and integrated individuals equipped with a high degree of social competence.[78] Another example is Montessori education, which is based on an educational environment tailored to basic human characteristics and to the individual personalities of each child.[79]

I strongly believe in the potential of all of us to learn and develop as individuals and that throughout our lives we should never stop learning, as we now understand that life-long learning actually shapes our brains. The important factor now is to enhance THE WAY we learn. As we connect more and more our understanding of the brain with how we as human beings learn, live and cohabit with each other, there is the hope that we will be able to understand how to shift forward into a new educational era: an educational era where learners are encouraged and supported at any age of their lives; where individuals are empowered and encouraged to be individualistic and to understand that everybody is different; where humans are able to apply lessons learnt to really support each other and to really live the vision of a harmonious, plentiful, peaceful life for all.

---

[78] For more on the Waldorf education approach, see www.waldorfeducation.org.
[79] For more on the Montessori Foundation, see www.montessori.org.

Above all, communication and language are key to our social interactions as humans. How we communicate can make all the difference.

Finally, I wish you all great success in your language coaching and learning and hope I inspire you to never ever stop coaching or learning languages.

'If you talk to a man in a language he understands, that goes to his head. If you talk to him in his language, that goes to his heart.'

– Nelson Mandela

ELC Neurolanguage Coaching® Certification Programme
ONLINE AND/OR FACE-TO-FACE

Become a Neurolanguage Coach

Accredited by the International Coach Federation

(with a total of 36 ICF accredited CCE hours)

This highly interactive online programme is divided into two parts:

- Module 1: Introduction to Coaching (3 two-hour online sessions)
- Module 2: Neurolanguage Coaching Skills – Bringing coaching and neuroscientific principles into the language learning process (15 two-hour online sessions)

Module 1: Introduction to coaching

This module focuses on introducing participants to coaching in general and also to the International Coaching Federation principles and core competencies. It also introduces an understanding of the theory and principles behind brain-based coaching and how neuroscientific research can assist in understanding and formulating powerful coaching conversations. This introduction aims to lay the pathway for participants to really assist and coach others to focus and develop themselves. Participants develop key coaching skills, such as active listening, powerful questioning and effective coaching conversations as well as learning to use different coaching models. Participants immediately start with coaching practice to pave the way for Module 2.

Learning outcomes:

- Sets the foundations for coaching and coaching conversations
- Deepens coaching effectiveness
- Enhances active listening and speaking skills
- Gives insights to various coaching models and develops their use in practice.

Module 2: Neurolanguage Coaching® skills

This module focuses on equipping participants with an understanding of the theory and principles behind language coaching and the ability to integrate principles of traditional coaching and brain-based coaching with the neuroscience of learning into the language learning process. Coaching models are practised and new language coaching models, as well as structure, are introduced.

The specific learning outcomes of Module 2 are as follows:

- How to use traditional coaching models in the language teaching process
- How to create the perfect learning state in the coachee based on principles of neuroscience
- How to connect language coaching to the ICF coaching competencies
- How to engage coaches into focused learning and sustain their goals with a high success rate
- How to connect and apply new language coaching models to the teaching process
- How to make the transformation from language teacher to language coach
- How to tailor make courses to the individual coachee.

Efficient Language Coaching® brings neuroscience and coaching into the learning process, as well as introducing new core 'language coaching' models and principles to provide a faster and more effective way of transferring language knowledge with sustainable effects.

The content covered is as follows:

- What is language coaching? What is it not?
- Coaching models – how to use them in language coaching
- Introducing the brain and principles of neuroscience
- What is the ideal learning state?
- Understanding how the coachee learns
- Applying coaching principles to language learning

- Applying coaching models to language learning
- Introducing new language coaching models/tools and how to use them
- How to structure language coaching sessions
- Administration of language coaching sessions
- Neurolanguage Coaching®
- Application of Neurolanguage Coaching® through the PACT PQC model – how to transmit grammar through powerful coaching conversations

Requirements

We ask you to provide proof of the following to enable you to participate on this course:

- Language teacher/trainer qualifications

and/or

- Demonstrated experience of language teaching (at least five years)

If you are already a 'coach' with a recognised coaching organisation, you only have to participate in Module 2, Neurolanguage Coaching. Please provide the necessary proof of teaching/professional qualifications as well as the coaching qualification.

Programme schedule

For the latest course schedule please refer to:

http://www.languagecoachingcertification.com/next-dates

Programme enquiries

For more information on our training, tuition fee and payment options, please visit our landing page at ELC at
www.languagecoachingcertification.com/book.

Note about the Author

Rachel M. Paling

Rachel Marie Paling founded Efficient Language Coaching® in 2008 and created the approach and method Neurolanguage Coaching® owning the registered trademark. Rachel started teaching English as a foreign language to adults in Spain over 30 years ago, when she was just 17. She lived in Spain for over 12 years and took the under-25s access to university exams with the UNED in Madrid and continued to study a Spanish Law degree for two years (in Spanish) then returned to the UK to continue her studies. After obtaining a BA Honours in Law and Spanish (with distinction in spoken Spanish) at the University of Sheffield (UK), she went on to do a Masters in Human Rights and Democratization (EMA) at the University of Padua in Italy and Ruhr-Universität Bochum in Germany. Throughout her ten years of studying, she gave language lessons to private individuals and worked with language schools. She qualified as a UK lawyer in 2003, but instead of pursuing a career as a lawyer, she combined her teaching experience, her specialisation in business English and her legal knowledge to coach top executives across Europe, also giving lectures in Legal English at the University of Verona for six years.

She has created the new method and approach called Neurolanguage Coaching® and has trained over 150 language teachers worldwide, certifying them as Neurolanguage coaches with her training course, one of the only language coaching certification courses in the world accredited by International Coach Federation USA.

This is Rachel's second book. Her first book is a children's book called *Chester The Vizla: I Believe in Miracles.*

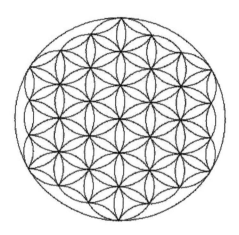